MW00534577

A CROWN THAT LASTS

YOU *ARE* NOT *YOUR* LABEL

DEMI LEIGH TEBOW

W Publishing Group
An Imprint of Thomas Nelson

A Crown That Lasts

Published in Nashville, Tennessee, by W Publishing, an imprint of Thomas Nelson.

Thomas Nelson titles may be purchased in bulk for educational, business, fundraising, or sales promotional use. For information, please email SpecialMarkets@ThomasNelson.com.

ISBN 978-1-4003-4361-4 (audiobook)
ISBN 978-1-4003-4360-7 (ePub)
ISBN 978-1-4003-4358-4 (HC)
ISBN 978-1-4003-4839-8 (ITPE)

Library of Congress Control Number: 2023945444

Printed in the United States of America

24 25 26 27 28 LBC 5 4 3 2 1

CONTENTS

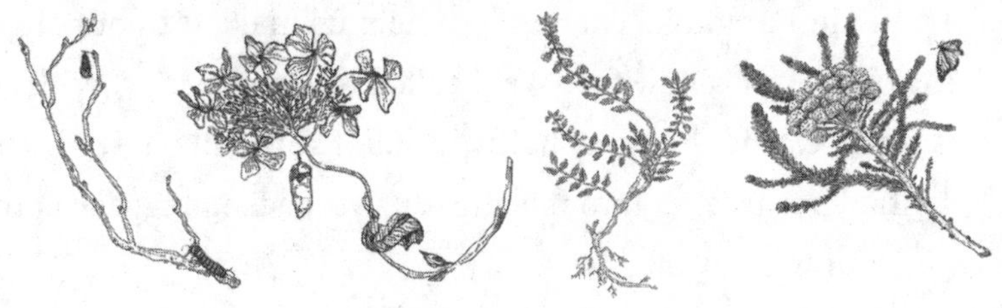

HI, FROM DEMI: HOW TO OPTIMIZE THIS BOOK

I'm crawling on the airport floor, trying to consolidate six suitcases of evening gowns, toiletries, underwear, and high heels into two suitcases while the guy of my dreams, who I'm hoping will one day propose to me, is watching the whole debacle unfold, embarrassed. To make matters worse, there are about twenty-seven people recording and taking pictures of this worst-case-nightmare-come-true situation. And I can feel my airbrushed makeup sweating off my stressed face.

If you're wondering how I got myself into this situation, it's pretty simple: I'd grabbed a bag; my brand-new boyfriend, Tim, had grabbed five; and we'd rushed to the airport to catch our international flight just two and a half hours before takeoff. My dream guy had cut a family trip to Israel short and flown halfway around the world to Thailand to cheer me on as I'd handed over my Miss Universe crown. We'd been dating for a few months at that point, and if I wasn't already smitten, his act of kindness definitely sealed the deal. Our driver had maneuvered through the crazy rush-hour traffic in Bangkok, Thailand, to help us make it to our flight back to South Africa on time. We'd rolled into the airport with six suitcases and clothes hanging halfway out of garment bags, which I had planned on stuffing into my already overpacked luggage at the check-in counter.

Less than an hour earlier, I'd handed over my crown and my title as Miss Universe on live TV. The Impact Arena where the event was hosted in Bangkok had been packed with thousands of people, and millions had watched the handover of the crown from their homes. So as we continued through the check-in process, people started recognizing me. I was still wearing a full face of airbrushed makeup, double-layered false lashes, and a head of big, bouncy pin curls from the live broadcast. Afterward, I'd only had time to throw on a mismatched track suit and some sneakers—honestly, I wore the first thing I could reach from the top of my suitcase—before leaving for the airport. Quite the odd picture.

I must have stood out like a tornado wearing a tutu. My six-foot-three handsome, athletic boyfriend didn't exactly fade into the masses either. People were crowding around the check-in counter, snapping photos of us, when one of my worst nightmares came true. The agent broke the news to me that my booking only allowed for *one* suitcase. To my despair, I had six! And almost all of them were over the weight limit. Because we were flying internationally, paying for extra bags, let alone overweight bags, was really expensive. So I figured that if I could spread the extra weight into Tim's suitcases, I would only have to pay the normal baggage price and not the fee for the extra weight.

Tim did his absolute best to be kind and patient, but we both knew this was about to get real embarrassing. I needed to open all of my suitcases—along with my new boyfriend's suitcases—on the airport floor and go to work. And friend, that's exactly what I did. I grabbed dresses and shirts, pantsuits and swimsuits, lotions and makeup galore, and started rearranging, shuffling, and stuffing them into Tim's exposed luggage all while trying not to accidentally fling out a bra or panty for what seemed like the entire airport to capture on video. I mean, I couldn't even make eye contact with Tim at this point! I was so mortified! The only item I couldn't figure out how to redistribute was my stack of forty Miss Universe programs, which weighed a ton.

You read that right, I had forty programs in my possession. Forty magazine-style programs that each weighed the same as a book, with my face all over them. After I'd handed over my crown, I'd grabbed as many of the hefty, shiny, Miss Universe programs as the production team would let me have. I'd given back my crown, my title, and my sash. Those programs were gold to me. They were the last thing I got to keep as Miss Universe. I was *not* leaving them behind in Thailand too.

Tim had a great idea. "Let's stuff them into my suit bag," he said confidently. A few fit in his suitcase, and the rest went into the suit bag as carry-on luggage. I realized that Tim deeply regretted this idea a few short minutes later when his biceps started cramping from awkwardly carrying the bag through the airport. I was just hoping that things weren't as bad as they seemed and that this guy I was still trying to win over would continue to like me back, with or without my Miss Universe programs.

My next hurdle was to hope that the security personnel wouldn't weigh our carry-on luggage at the baggage checkpoint. I tried my best not to make eye contact as they scanned our bags because I couldn't let them see my guilty countenance. Tim tried his best to carry three-dozen bulky booklets as if they weighed nothing more than a suit. To our relief, we made it through security without alarming anyone. But as soon as Tim picked up the heavy garment bag full of the stowaway programs from the security conveyer belt, the bottom ripped out. Suddenly, the airport floor was awash in shiny program booklets all featuring my face.

The last little drops of my previous identity printed on glossy paper with a big, bold label—MISS UNIVERSE—were physically scattered all over the airport floor. At this point, Tim became a saint! We were both down on our hands and knees, crawling around and grabbing the books as quickly as possible before they drew even more attention. We weren't fast enough though. Before I could grab them all and stuff them back into the torn suit bag, someone yelled, "Oh my word! Is that you? Miss Universe?" I just kept silent and thought, *No, I am no longer Miss Universe. My identity is just as torn up as this garment bag and feels just as scattered as these books on this airport floor.* I had handed over my crown, and with it a giant part of myself, and I wasn't sure yet how to get it back.

YOUR TURN

I don't know what your story is, but I'm guessing you haven't been down on your hands and knees in an airport recently, scooping up your own face. But my hope is that we can connect through the familiar pieces of our stories. You don't need to have lost your job as Miss Universe to have struggled with an identity crisis. You only need to open your phone, get that call from the doctor's office, have a loved one cut you off, a calling fail, a dream collapse, a love die, a degree tank, a last child graduate, or a cross-country move to leave you stranded and starting all over again to be confused about who you are. Take it from the girl who literally dropped her sense of purpose and watched her identity slip through her fingers. My prayer is that through these stories you'll feel less alone and discover practical steps for how to figure out who you are again, what really matters and what doesn't, and what to do when you're stuck in the messy middle. Let's keep growing together.

On that note, this book is divided into four parts: Dig, Plant, Grow, and Flourish. Here's how to maximize what you get out of them:

Part 1: Dig—In chapters 1, 2, and 3, you're going to recognize the origin of confidence and learn how to unpack your past so you can better understand yourself. This phase is the initial introspection or exploration phase. It will involve us digging into our pasts together, understanding our roots, and unraveling the elements that formed our identities—perhaps uncovering aspects that might not have been beneficial or sustainable in the long run.

Part 2: Plant—In chapters 4 and 5, you're going to learn about seeking out and saying yes to mission-focused opportunities, even if it feels scary. This section focuses on how to do the hard work of managing your time, energy, and resources with optimal priorities so you can cultivate optimal growth. This phase signifies a period of deliberate action. After digging and uncovering the root aspects, planting new seeds or ideas might involve consciously choosing what to nurture and cultivate within yourself. Together we will learn to plant seeds of new values, habits, or perspectives that align with a more sustainable and fulfilling identity.

Part 3: Grow—In chapters 6, 7, and 8, you will understand that platform, ability, and skill are pathways to *promote* purpose, not purpose itself. Once the seeds are planted, you'll need to embrace the process of patiently nurturing and allowing those newly planted ideas or values to develop and eventually flourish. It involves personal development, continuous learning, and gradual growth that will allow you to eventually morph into your everlasting identity.

Part 4: Flourish—In chapters 9 and 10, you'll be challenged to see life through the lens of eternity and your work as an opportunity for eternal impact. Flourishing is a continual, lifelong process. Together, we're going to continue to persevere through the good times and the hard ones. This final section suggests the culmination of the process—the flourishing of the newly cultivated aspects of your identity. It symbolizes your thriving era where you have successfully untangled your identity from beliefs, titles, or experiences that were only temporary. From here, you can grow into a more authentic and sustainable version of yourself.

Friend, thank you for accepting my invitation to walk beside you, or maybe it's more appropriate to say *unpack* and *sort through* your luggage together while you come face-to-face with your own identity—all the pieces of it you're trying to make sense of. It's okay to unpack all your baggage full of built-up uncertainty here with me. I've been there. It's messy, but it means you're going to get the chance to honestly pull back the curtain on your dreams and struggles, wins and losses, joy and fears. The exciting part is that you will figure out, all over again, who you are and why your life, with all its ups and downs, matters so very much.

PART ONE

DIG

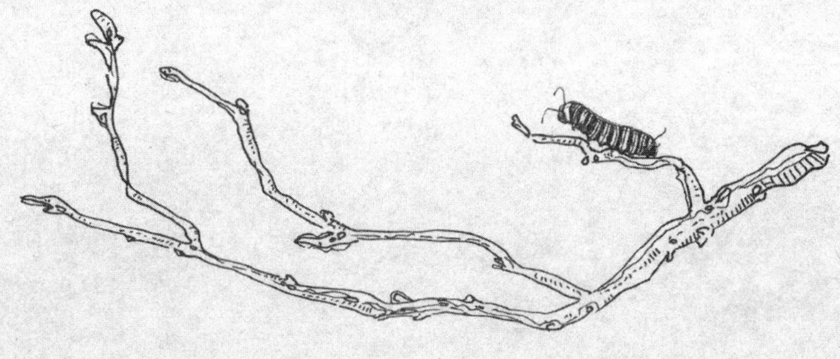

Taste and see that the LORD *is good.*
How happy is the person who takes refuge in him!
You who are his holy ones, fear the LORD*,*
for those who fear him lack nothing.

PSALM 34:8–9 (CSB)

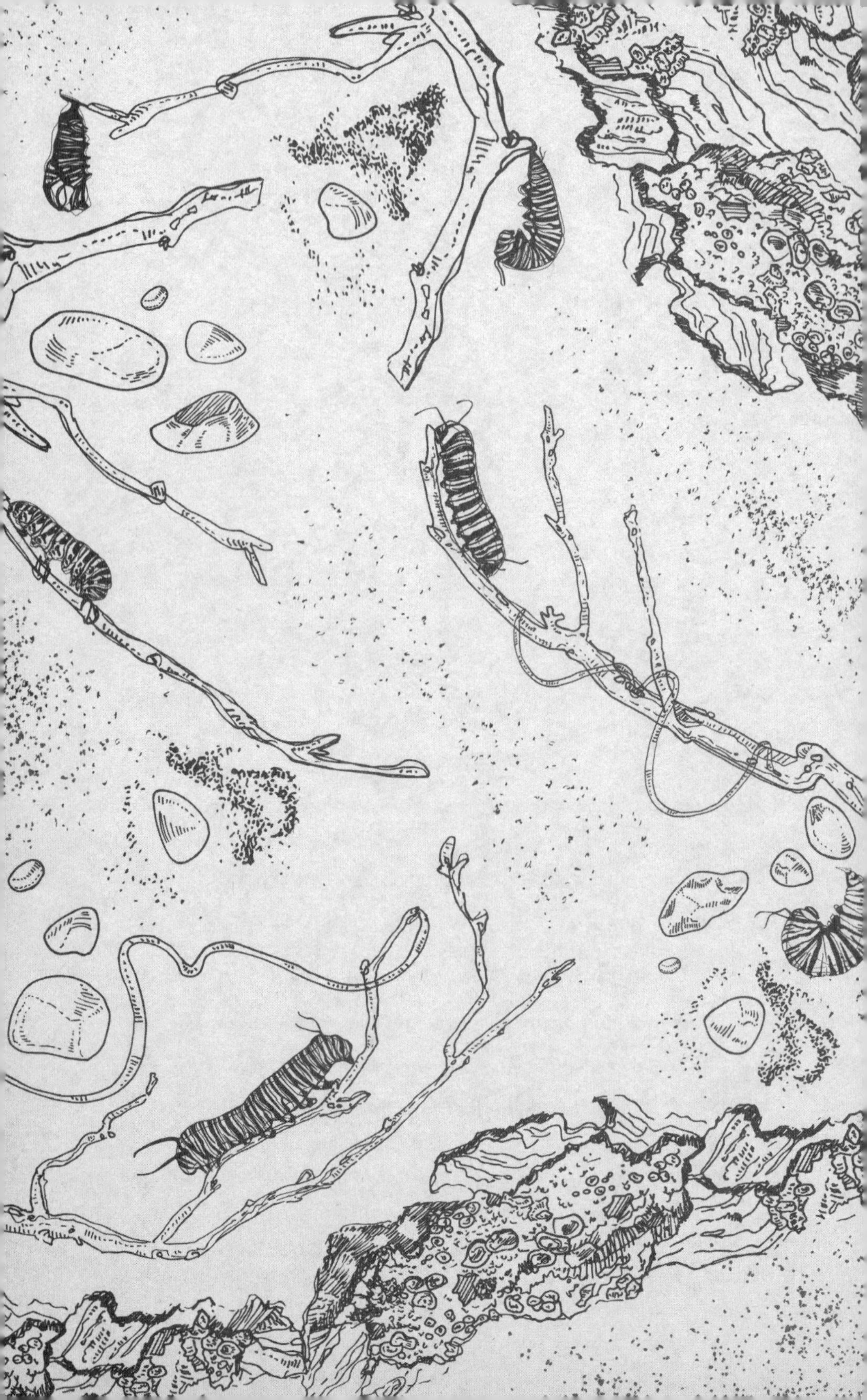

In Plato's *Republic*, Socrates famously said, "We are discussing no small matter, but how we ought to live." *How* we live is important, but understanding what drives how we live is equally important. In chapters 1 through 3, we will "dig" into our pasts to make better sense of who we are to set up where we're going. We'll dive into the common issue of tying our confidence to the wrong things. Next, we'll face the reality that life doesn't always go according to our well-crafted plans. And finally, we'll tackle the frustration of feeling stuck and stagnant in "waiting" seasons.

Each chapter in this dig section gives you the opportunity to do some hard work and perhaps confront some buried pain or make peace with uncertainty. As you'll find out, my story is full of unanswered questions, unmet expectations, and moments of insecurity. But over the last several years, as I have taken steps to dig, I've discovered that although rebuilding or refining your identity is difficult, it opens a door to finally trust God's goodness and sets yourself up for what matters most.

In these chapters, my hope is that you'll:

- Recognize the origin of your confidence.
- Identify unreliable identity labels and replace them with truth.
- Embrace God's timing in order to develop a mindset that chooses to trust despite disappointments.
- Be willing to take action and wait on God's timing.

- Understand the power of what a few seconds of compassion can do for people.
- Appreciate the God-wink moments and allow them to propel you forward.

ONE

UNTANGLE YOUR IDENTITY FROM YOUR LABEL

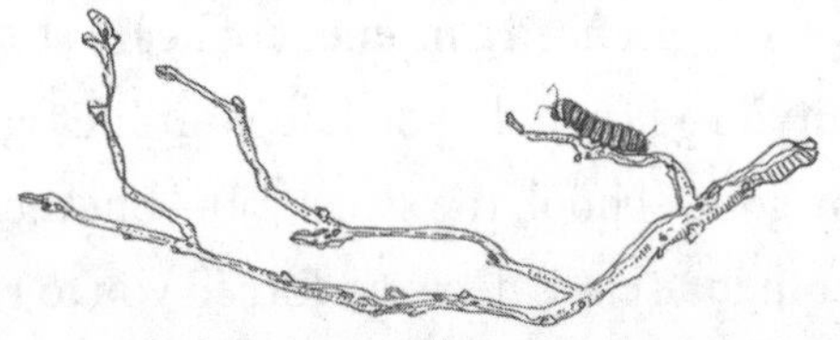

"Take your first walk as Miss Universe!" Steve Harvey bellowed over the thundering chorus of cheers and applause. As Miss Philippines turned to face the cheering audience and walk down the runway and into her new life, I spun in the opposite direction. My year as Miss Universe had officially come to an end.

The hundred-thousand-plus green and yellow Swarovski crystals encrusting the custom-made Gert-Johan Coetzee gown that draped my body faded into a dull silhouette as I walked into the shadows behind the curtain. My entire support team—a full-time manager, security guard, videographer, social media manager, and stylist, to name just a few—whooshed past me to get to their new job, the *new* Miss Universe. It felt like I had become part of the scenery.

Shoot! What do I do now? Do I just wait here? Will someone come to get me? Someone always comes to get me, I tried to reassure myself. *I'll wait here. Surely someone will be back for me soon.*

By the time the crowd started exiting the building, I reckoned I should probably find my own way back to my dressing room. But I couldn't remember which direction it was since I'd been escorted backstage by my team before my final walk as Miss Universe. I hadn't been paying attention to where I was being taken because I trusted that the team always had things under control. Then when the show was over, everything went from being fine to my world being flipped upside down in a matter of seconds. And I didn't even see it coming.

Have you ever experienced a moment of heart-stopping, sweaty-palms uncertainty? You thought you had your life figured out—the right friends, the good school, the sweet job—but then a transition, a diagnosis, or someone else's decision forced you to reevaluate who you are and where you're going? Have you ever been completely blindsided by a situation? Perhaps a relationship ended and your whole identity had gotten caught up in being a girlfriend, a bride-to-be, a wife. Maybe you were starting another completely average week when the doctor's office called and changed everything. Or you were caught off guard by not getting that job or *any* job after spending years in college getting all the right qualifications you thought you needed to succeed.

The end of my reign as Miss Universe was my rug-ripped-from-underneath-my-six-inch-heels moment. I had dedicated years of my life working toward that goal, and it was suddenly over in the space of the one minute and twenty-two seconds it took for me to do my farewell walk. When I turned around, I found I had no idea what to do or where to go next. It's a scary experience to be stranded in a future that is no longer clear. It's filled with doubt, questions, anxiety, and in my case, an identity crisis.

I had left something on stage that night. And it wasn't just the Miss Universe crown I had passed on to that year's rightful owner. It was what I had attached to the crown, the one adorned with 500 diamonds and 120 pearls on a delicate frame that glistened and glowed and represented a future I thought I understood. It was my identity. My source of confidence. I didn't know I had lost both at the time. And I didn't realize it was a false identity that I had lost. A false sense of confidence birthed from the promises, dreams, and expectations of achieving something I'd always wanted.

So as I thrust myself into the logistics of finding my way through the backstage maze, the anxiety-drenched question lingered: *What am I going to do now? I guess get out of this dress, find Tim, and make it to my flight back home departing in three hours.* As I went through the motions of slinking out of—and returning—my dress, changing, and heading out to catch the flight home to South Africa, the chaos overwhelmed an unnamable emptiness. I knew two things that night: One, I was returning to my homeland. Two, I had no idea what I was going to do next.

But before I unpack how I ended up on a plane with no crown, no team, and no clue what to do next, you need to know how I arrived at that night in the first place.

BLOOD, SWEAT, AND HIGH HEELS

When I was a young girl growing up in the small coastal town of Sedgefield in the Western Cape province of South Africa, my mom and I would switch on our TV, the old big-box kind, an hour early to make sure we caught the live broadcast of the Miss South Africa competition every year. The opening scene, usually consisting of a choreographed dance, and the question-and-answer rounds were my favorite. During every elimination round, I sat on the edge of my seat holding my thumbs (the South African version of fingers crossed) for my favorite candidate to advance. My mom and I loved watching; it was our little tradition.

I was mesmerized by the sparkling ball gowns, Cinderella-like shoes, and the "happily ever after" story of a winner walking away looking like a real-life princess with an elaborate prize package. *She gets her hair done for free for a year! What a dream*! I thought. My mom and I loved following the winner's journey after the crowning. Many former Miss South Africa winners have succeeded post-reign in becoming successful entrepreneurs, business owners, philanthropists, TV personalities, and essentially great role models.

As I matured, I realized that the true beauty of a Miss South Africa is not found in her sparkling objects or temporary fame; instead, it is anchored in empathy and authenticity, which touches not only the eye but also the hearts and minds of those who experience it. True beauty defies conventional norms and remains timeless, leaving a lasting impact on the observer's consciousness. That's the type of woman I grew up aspiring to be, a Miss South Africa–type of woman. And I was willing to put in the work to get there. A common theme running throughout my life is that I am always diligent and dedicated to the hard work required to reach a goal. At school I was a B student and usually ended up on the B team in sports. However, I ranked an A in competitiveness, stubbornness, and not taking no for an answer. My husband, Tim, can attest to this. Making the first team or getting an A average was never something that just fell into my lap. It took practicing for hours on my own after the team had already gone home. It took waking up early in the morning to go for an extra three-mile run before school. It took tutoring, long study sessions, and extra after-school classes to get my As. Working for what I wanted became my default. If I wanted nice things, I had to earn them, including the title of Miss South Africa and eventually Miss Universe.

It's easy to assume the prettiest face with the prettiest dress gets the title. From experience, I can assure you that is not the case. Physical beauty was merely a facet of the journey. The lasting beauty lies in one's ability to inspire, uplift, and empower others. That was what we were ultimately judged on. Thousands of girls entered Miss South Africa 2017. Pageants as a whole can be a lengthy and taxing process. Competing for my national title took more than six months of interviews, completing tasks and tests, doing media appearances, traveling all over the country, taking part in philanthropic work, and participating in fitness challenges.

With social media becoming an aspect of the competition, I was constantly on guard and aware of having sixty million South Africans eyes on me. They watched and judged my every move, outfit, and conversation to determine if I was fit for the title. Because the Miss South Africa organization made use of a public voting system to help determine the winner, the country's opinion mattered. I navigated the weight of pleasing a nation while trying to balance work, finishing my degree in business management and entrepreneurship, and overcoming everyday life obstacles like navigating adulthood.

A piece of advice my mom gave me that still echoes in my memory is, "Demi, no matter what you do, make sure you do it well. If you clean up after your dog, then do it well. If you become an actress, then know your script better than anyone else. If you clean homes for a living, then make sure they are the cleanest homes in the world." In essence, what she taught me was to always strive for excellence. My approach to winning Miss South Africa was no different from my approach to cleaning up after our dog, achieving As as a B student, or making the A-team in sports as a B-level athlete. I was committed to working harder than anyone else.

During my time as Miss South Africa, I had the opportunity to represent my home country on an international stage to compete for the Miss Universe title. Since it was an opportunity that I would never have a second chance at, I decided to take drastic steps to achieve drastic results.

I stopped speaking Afrikaans, my native language, for a few months to better my English. I hired a life coach, a pageant coach, a personal trainer, and a public speaking coach to assist me in competing at the highest level. I had a rigorous schedule that was organized to the minute. Like an athlete in training, it included everything from when I needed to eat to when it was time to go to sleep. It even included walking in high heels for twelve hours some days. Looking at my bunion toe, I admit that I completely overdid that part.

I hired makeup artists and hairstylists to teach me how to appear perfect every day. This was important because once you arrive at Miss Universe, you have no access to your team; you are completely on your own. That includes doing your own hair and makeup every day with the exception of prelims, the final night, and any sponsored photoshoots. Call me the "queen of pin curls" if you want; they became one of my secret talents. I still can't apply fake eyelashes, however, so I taught myself how to apply a sharp liquid liner to create an illusion of lashes.

The Miss South Africa team held impromptu interview sessions where they drilled me on current world affairs. This helped me stay on my toes and on top of relevant topics. Once you arrive at Miss Universe, you encounter media and judges from every corner of the world, and the interview topics are completely unknown. Being underprepared was not an option. My coach and I decided that if I made it to the top ten, we would do a drastic change and put my hair into a top knot bun. Most girls usually keep their hair down for that portion of the competition, but we wanted to be different and constantly looked for ways to stand out.

During onstage rehearsals, I estimated what the TV time-out period would be after the top ten got announced. I calculated that I would have four or so minutes to get backstage, change out of my bathing suit, put my hair into a sleek top knot bun, change my shoes and earrings, and get back on stage for the evening wear portion. Yikes! I'm sweating just thinking about how fast that turnaround time is. I would go back to my room after rehearsals and practice doing all the above in under four minutes. Once I knew what music we were going to walk to onstage, I downloaded it and listened to the track on repeat, closing my eyes and visualizing stepping onto the stage. I'd even remind myself that the stage would be slippery and not to be caught off guard by it. I memorized where the cameras would appear to ensure I made eye contact because the judges watch a screen with the live broadcast instead of watching the actual stage. I had everything down to a science to be as well-prepared as possible to give myself the best chance of winning. I wasn't going to take any chances with losing out on my one shot.

COUNTDOWN TO THE CROWN

Lights, cameras, action! The final show was about to start. I was shaking from adrenaline and excitement because I knew I could walk onto that stage with contentment and truly enjoy the moment regardless of the outcome. It's that feeling of being so proud of how far you've come because you know you've given it your all. I was emotional thinking that I was one of only a few dozen women from my country to ever walk that stage. I slipped my "South Africa" sash over my gold dress, fixed my lippie one more time, and silently told myself, *You go, girl! You've got this! This is the moment you've worked for your whole life!*

When the top sixteen got announced and I was the last candidate to make it into the regional cut, my nerves were strung so tight. But being nervous only meant that I cared—cared about representing my home country well and not wasting a monumental moment. South Africa hadn't won a Miss Universe title in thirty-nine years. This was my chance, but it was also South Africa's chance. The top ten got announced, then the top five, and lastly the top three.

I made it!

Steve Harvey heightened the tension when he said, "The night began with ninety-two of the world's most impressive women. And now we've narrowed it down to three. Each of these finalists have shown they all deserve to carry the title, but only one of them is about to become Miss Universe."[1]

Surely it doesn't end here? I didn't come this far to come only this far. It's not over till it's over, I told myself. Steve Harvey called out the second runner-up, leaving only me and Miss Colombia remaining. We took center stage. The last spot remained. Steve got ready to announce the winner as the dramatic music played. I held Miss Colombia's hands, and we wished each other well as we waited hopefully. I remember telling myself with a content heart and the biggest smile, *Girl, you couldn't have done anything else to earn this title.* Win or not, my heart was full because I knew my Creator had already penned my destiny. If this achievement was meant to weave into the larger tapestry of His design for my life, it wouldn't slip through His hands. My cheeks hurt because I couldn't stop smiling. I was in awe of what God had allowed me to be a part of.

"One of you is about to become our new Miss Universe," Steve continued. "If for any reason the winner cannot fulfill her duties, the first runner-up will take her place. Good luck to you both."

Steve looked at the card and announced, "The new Miss Universe is . . . South Africa! Congratulations! Take your first walk as Miss Universe!"

I gasped, held my hand in front of my mouth, and looked around to triple check I had heard correctly. When someone from the organization draped a sash over my shoulders and handed me a bouquet of colorful flowers, I knew my little-girl dream had come true. I had just become the sixty-sixth Miss Universe. My predecessor walked toward me carrying a crown with a seven-feather design, encrusted with 500 diamonds and 120 South Sea and Akoya pearls. When I saw the crown, it immediately felt like a God-wink moment. You know, one of those moments where you have no doubt that God's hand was in it all along. Pearls happen to be my birthstone.

Being content in that moment before the winner got announced didn't mean I would have been fine with losing. I was still a girl with a dream who cared deeply and had worked hard to get to this moment. But it also meant that I would've been able to walk off that stage at peace, knowing I gave it my everything. While I would have been disappointed about the outcome, I also knew that if it was meant for me, it wouldn't have missed me. Winning was not only a personal victory but a tribute to the rich South African identity that I am honored to represent. So it felt like a victory for each young girl from a small town somewhere in South Africa with a big dream.

No matter how hard I tried, I couldn't stop smiling. I was so amazed at what had just happened, and my brain couldn't process it all fast enough. Neither could my cell phone. By the time I reached my room to check in with everyone back home in South Africa, I couldn't get my phone to turn on. I had gained just under a million new followers in a few hours, and nobody had thought to warn me about turning my notifications off. My phone's charge couldn't keep up with the momentum of new follower notifications. I've heard of people experiencing overnight success; that was literally the case for me.

WHO ARE YOU?

After I was crowned, my manager was the first person to meet me as I came off stage. I'll never forget her first words to me: "Hi, who are you?" I was wearing my new sash across my chest with bold, sparkly letters proclaiming "Miss Universe" and a crown on my head no one could miss. So I responded with the less obvious, "My name is Demi." She asked the same question again, so I responded, "I'm Miss South Africa." Shaking her head and declaring no, she asked me one last time, "Who are you?" And then it clicked. "I am Miss Universe," I proclaimed. She grabbed me by the hand and said, "Great, Miss Universe, let's get to work."

I immediately got whisked away to take photos with media on center stage, followed by a quick makeup touch-up and water break before a press conference with media from all over the world. I got asked questions ranging from how to be confident to how I was planning on solving the water crisis in Cape Town. Not kidding. Then it was time for my first official portrait and group photos with sponsors. Once that was done, my bags got moved into the penthouse suite where I had a few minutes to catch up with my family. After that, I managed to sleep for three hours before leaving for the airport to catch a flight to New York City, my home for the next year. Most of my year as Miss Universe was a very beautiful, very meaningful, and very well-managed rat race.

I had over twenty international trips that year since we visited some countries multiple times. My apartment was provided, the car service was always on time, my stylist planned my outfits well in advance, my personal trainer wrote up my workouts, my visa applications were taken care of, my apartment manager always had the fridge stocked, and my laundry was picked up weekly. If you've ever lived in New York City, you'll know what a luxury it is to have your laundry done! That year was unlike any year I had ever experienced before or since. I just had to show up.

Since I'd grown up working so hard for everything I wanted, "just showing up" was out of my comfort zone. But as you can imagine, it was something I got used to very quickly. Showing up became my new norm. My doorman greeted me as Miss Universe. At appearances I was introduced as Miss Universe. Even my luggage got labeled as Miss Universe. At first it was cute and fun and exciting, but then slowly, without my realizing it, I *became* the title. Soon, my identity was rooted in the crown on my head and the label across my chest.

My year as Miss Universe was an experience I will cherish forever. I could write a whole book about all the lessons I learned and value I gained from those 365 days. It's a year that without question contributed to shaping the woman I am today. I believe I am better today than I would've been without that experience. I am a better public speaker. I have a better understanding of cultures and countries around the world. I have a broadened perspective on business and different industries. I have stretched my perspective on what I thought my capabilities are. I have the experience of living outside of my home country. I got to witness and experience the needs people have worldwide. And I learned that you do not need to speak someone's language to communicate compassion.

However, the day I was dreading but had always known was coming inevitably arrived. And none of my hard work, diligence, or pageant preparations could have prepared me for it or for what would follow. When I competed for the crown, I knew every detail of the process. I had researched previous contests; therefore, the order of events was familiar. But I never once thought to research what happens *after* you give the crown back, or what happens *after* you reach your goal or achieve your dreams.

It's kind of like the transition from college to real life. You show up on your first day of school and, even though you're a little disoriented, you know what's supposed to happen next. You have a schedule, pick up your books, attend class, take exams, do internships, eventually graduate, and apply for a job. After that, nobody really talks you through what happens when you get your first job and move into your first apartment. Nobody walks you through getting medical insurance or how to pay your taxes for the first time. Not to mention the oil change you didn't know your car needed two years ago.

After crowning my successor, I walked off that stage and nobody noticed. I had no idea what came next. Eventually, I found my way back to my dressing room and changed out of my sleek Swarovski crystal dress into a more comfortable outfit and walkable shoes; the little bit of identity I had left I put in the dress bag. Later at the airport before my flight I washed away my confidence with makeup remover.

Have you ever rooted your identity in a day-to-day task, routine, goal, or another person? Perhaps you are a mom who's an empty nester for the first time, and your focus of the last eighteen years is suddenly a few hundred miles away, making their own lunch and driving themselves to their own appointments. What are you waking up to every day after you just sold the business you've been building for the last ten years? Who are you when the person you loved stops loving you back? When the goal you've worked years for is met or maybe disappoints? When the job you've spent more than half your life at is over or pushes you out? When your most comfortable, most familiar label falls away, who are you? What do you do next when what you had to show up for every day is no longer there?

I've often heard people who are facing retirement say that they're scared because they don't know what they'll do with all the extra time on their hands. Walking off that stage was like a kind of retirement for me. I understand that this might sound strange to some of you. You might be thinking that once you walk away with a title like Miss Universe, your future will be filled with realized dreams and endless opportunities. It's certainly what I thought as a young girl entranced by the televised version of Miss Universe. And before competing, a friend had told me, "When you win that title, you will never have to wonder about the next opportunity." Turns out, like most things in life, that isn't quite how reality unfolds.

Of course, the crown creates endless opportunities for all former title holders, including myself. But there's a distinction between wearing the title and *becoming* the title. And there's a danger when you start to take your identity from the crown. For a full year, the reason I was sought after to attend events and do the commercials or receive the awards was not because of my value and worth as an individual but because of the value attached to the label I wore. I became a vessel for an agenda. When there's no longer an agenda, the vessel is no longer needed. Even though the average Boeing 747 is worth approximately $418 million, they become worthless when grounded as they were when the whole world shut down. Borders closed and there were no passengers to fly anywhere.

It wasn't handing back the title or the fact that I was no longer the number one girl in the universe that crushed me. It was the fact that I had attached my identity to a temporary crown. What hit me in the face like a ton of bricks was that when I passed it on, I handed over my identity, confidence, value, worth, and what I thought was a big part of my life's purpose along with the crown that used to be on my head.

ANCHOR YOUR IDENTITY TO MORE THAN YOUR LABEL

About a year and a half after I handed over the Miss Universe title, I was, in all honesty, still feeling lost and confused about my life's purpose. But I remember the specific moment when I realized for the first time that even though I didn't have it all figured out, I could find a peace regardless. A few months after Tim and I were married, we were asked to do a joint Q&A onstage. We walked out and sat down on a soft velvet couch center stage. Tim grabbed my shaking hand and held it tight. I wasn't nervous about speaking in front of a full auditorium and to thousands of people live streaming the interview. I was nervous because I still had no idea who I was but felt like I was expected to have my life mapped out for the interview. I tried memorizing the answers to the questions we'd been provided beforehand, but my nerves took over. It felt like my operating system was frozen, like when a computer freezes and gives you nothing but a "loading" screen. Have you ever tried opening a file in your mind and just blanked? It's such a terrible feeling.

Tim and I were asked a few questions. My plan was to have Tim answer as many as possible. *Heck, let him answer them all*, I thought. It was going relatively well since I was able to latch a few words onto some of what Tim was saying, until a question was finally aimed directly at me.

"Demi, you're known for your beauty. You're known for winning these pageants. I see a culture that sends messages to women of all ages saying they're not enough. I'd love for you just to talk to us for a few minutes about what true beauty is and how you see that."

True beauty. You're not enough. Worth. Confidence. Come on, file! Open! I know the right answer. I freaked out! It felt like I was back in school, staring at an exam page, knowing I'd memorized the answer but just couldn't recall it. We might memorize Scripture like we memorize the formula for solving a math problem, but memorizing doesn't always equal understanding. I knew that God knew me by name, He had a plan for my life, and I was filled with infinite value. How did I know this? Because I had read it in Scripture. However, I didn't believe it at the moment because I couldn't see that plan practically applied to my life.

I recalled Psalm 139:13–15: *Fearfully and wonderfully made. That's a good one.* It's always been a go-to verse for me. *I can make something of this answer,* I assured myself. In my heart I wasn't looking for the right answer; I was looking for the honest answer. The moment I started talking, trying to answer the question while truly having no idea what was about to come out of my mouth, the Lord showed up in my heart. He allowed me to answer that question not just for the audience, but for myself.

When I was set to go and compete for Miss Universe, there were ninety-two countries competing. Being five six, I was one of the shortest girls to ever compete for that title. People started placing me in a box, saying, "She won't win because she's too short." They started defining my future according to my height. Even though I know that's absurd, back then it was hard for their words not to get anchored in my head. I know that in this day and age, many young girls also get put into boxes based on how social media defines them, or based on a single trait, talent, stumble, or mistake.

As a believer, I've had to go back and define self-love, self-worth, and self-image to myself. Psalm 139:13–15 says that we are "fearfully and wonderfully made . . . knit together in our mother's womb." I love the word *knit*. It reminds me of how my grandmother used to knit me little jerseys. We call them jerseys in South Africa, but you call them sweaters in the United States. Grandma would make the most beautiful patterns. One of my favorite jerseys she made was red with a black-and-white panda bear on it. While we were on holiday together, she spent days knitting that jersey, pulling it loose, rethreading it, making sure it was perfect. She even sewed little eyes onto the panda bear's face to make it look real. Her act of love made me realize that God knit us together in our mother's womb even more carefully than my grandmother could ever knit that jersey. Just like my grandmother planned out her patterns and blocked her designs to the inch, God also has a precise plan for our lives. He created us in love, by love, and for love. If that does not make you feel worthy, I don't think any amount of makeup, money, clothes, titles, awards, followers, or praise will ever make you feel worthy.

When we define self-confidence, we will realize that it is rooted in the temporary, just like the crown I eventually had to give back. It is evident that our self-confidence will run dry at some point, but God's love for us is everlasting and unchanging.

That day and that interview marked a turning point for me. My waiting season wasn't over yet. My life still felt split between two continents, and I wasn't exactly sure what came next. But I chose to remember who had made me, and with that assurance came a new type of confidence.

SELF-CONFIDENCE IS SUPERFICIAL

Our English word *confidence* comes from a fourteenth-century Latin word meaning "to have full trust."[2] Using this definition, *self-confidence* would then mean "to have full trust in oneself." That is what the crown provided me. Self-confidence, by definition, is fully relying on yourself as an individual. You become central in making all decisions and judgments based on the "full trust" you have in yourself—whatever comes your way! I don't know about you, but no matter how much I try to muster up *trust* inside of *myself*, I eventually fall short and find myself in a situation where I doubt my own ability, judgment, control, and power. This isn't always a bad thing; it just means I'm human. Looking back, I now realize why having full trust in oneself is not maintainable. It can lead to a host of negative things, such as:

- *Overconfidence*: Lack of humility and overestimating one's abilities or knowledge can result in poor decision-making, overpromising, and underdelivering.
- *Dismissal of Feedback*: Rejecting constructive criticism due to the belief that you are always right hinders the personal growth and development that comes from wise counsel.
- *Lack of Adaptability*: It is harder to adjust, approach, or learn new skills when needed.
- *Underestimating Challenges*: Underestimating the complexities of a situation might cause you to take action without fully understanding potential negative outcomes.
- *Failure to Seek Help*: With excessive self-confidence, you begin to believe you can and should be able to handle everything on your own, resulting in burnout.
- *Stubbornness*: With an unwillingness to see things from a different perspective, you are always "dying on the hill" of your opinion.
- *Insecurity When Failure Occurs*: Self-worth that is closely tied to your performance is unhealthy.

- *Fickle Emotions*: Self-confidence is rooted in a feeling . . . and feelings fade.

Although the basic psychological premise of self-confidence can produce healthy and positive outcomes as it relates to mental health, risk-taking, building relationships, academic performance, and such, if we put our *full* trust in ourselves, we will ultimately be let down (or let others down). While self-confidence has its benefits and value, what I have learned is that relying on self-confidence alone for your identity is unsustainable.

GOD-CONFIDENCE IS SOUL DEEP

I propose a different type of confidence not based on our ego but rooted in Someone who is all-powerful, all-knowing, always present, and unchanging! A person worthy of attaching our identity to: God. I call this type of confidence "God-confidence." And the definition is simple: to have *full trust in who God is*!

King Solomon of Israel, one of the wisest men to ever walk the earth, wrote in Proverbs 3:5–6:

> Trust in the LORD with all your heart
> And do not lean on your own understanding.
> In all your ways acknowledge Him,
> And He will make your paths straight (NASB).

To have full trust in *who God is* leaves no room for trust in the self. You can only take *you* so far! Since our labels are always changing, we need a source of permanence in which to anchor our identity, a rock that we can build our confidence on. God-confidence echoes

David in Psalm 145:3, "The LORD is
greatness is unsearchable" (CSB
control and believes that God is
than you and me and the circumstan
confidence acknowledges that He is "a
understanding is infinite" (Psalm 147:5 NA
God provides assurance, hope, purpose, and cou
our challenges.

But God-confidence isn't just about believing in His
it's also about understanding His *goodness*. Always. To hav
trust in God means you are rooted in knowing His goodness an
His promises. He is not just a promise-maker but a promise-keeper. The Bible contains so many promises that God has made to His people. Here are some of my favorites:

- *Gift of salvation*: "For God so loved the world that he gave his one and only Son, that whoever believes in him shall not perish but have eternal life" (John 3:16).
- *God's presence*: "Be content with what you have, for he has said, 'I will never leave you nor forsake you'" (Hebrews 13:5 ESV).
- *Purpose in life on earth*: "For we are his workmanship, created in Christ Jesus for good works, which God prepared beforehand, that we should walk in them" (Ephesians 2:10 ESV).
- *Guidance and wisdom*: "If any of you lacks wisdom, let him ask God, who gives generously to all without reproach, and it will be given him" (James 1:5 ESV).
- *Free from shame*: "There is therefore now no condemnation for those who are in Christ Jesus" (Romans 8:1 ESV).
- *Continuous development*: "He who began a good work in you will perfect it until the day of Christ Jesus" (Philippians 1:6 NASB1995).

erhaps my *most* favorite:

God's inseparable love: "For I am sure that neither death nor life, nor angels nor rulers, nor things present nor things to come, nor powers, nor height nor depth, nor anything else in all creation, will be able to separate us from the love of God in Christ Jesus our Lord" (Romans 8:38–39 ESV).

When we step back and realize the *greatness* and *goodness* of God, putting our full trust in anything else seems silly—whether it's a career, a relationship, a label, or a crown. When your emotions are fickle, God is steadfast! When your understanding is limited, He is omnipotent! When you feel insecure, your value and worth in His eyes doesn't budge! When you are overwhelmed, His peace provides hope! When you feel like you don't have what it takes, He has overcome the world! When push comes to shove, self-confidence can only take you so far, which is why being rooted in God-confidence is the only way to live. Let's exchange our superficial self-confidence for a supernatural God-confidence and root ourselves in a crown and an identity that will last for all of eternity.

TWO

WORK THROUGH THE WAIT

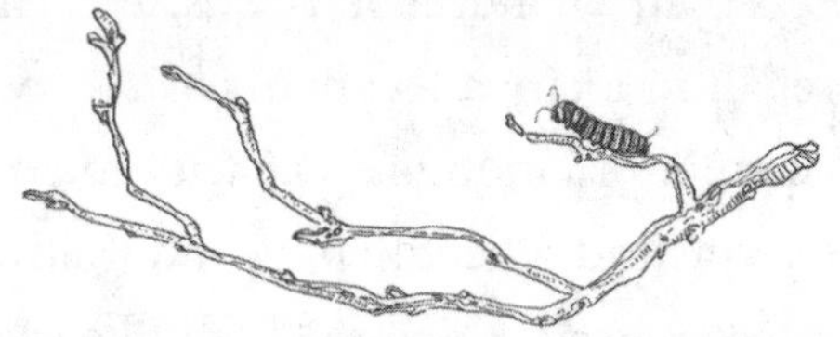

When I handed over my Miss Universe crown, I didn't realize I was entering a waiting season until it was nearly over. It just felt like life was miserable; everything was hard, and the slightest amount of success required endless effort. I was unsure of where to live—and by that I don't just mean which neighborhood or city or even which state to live in. I mean which *continent*. I thought about moving back to South Africa to live with my family, but on the other hand my fiancé was in the United States, and I knew it would become our home. I figured I might as well start building a life in America for myself post–Miss Universe.

Tim and I had decided early on in our relationship that we didn't want to move in together until we were married. Even though it could have simplified many things in my life, I have never regretted that decision. But everything I owned was spread across four different cities in two different countries. I lost track of what I had and where it was stored, and I could never find what I was looking for.

I had no state ID, so I couldn't open my own cell phone account, and I had a really hard time getting a lease for an apartment. I dealt with expiring visas and the many policies and procedures that come with that. Also, I was still feeling run down from hopping between continents the previous year as Miss Universe. Even though the travels were fun, jet lag was not. I dealt with side effects like exhaustion, physical weakness, a weakened immune system, brain fog, and a lack of appetite for months.

I had no constant, no routine, and was operating on a day-to-day basis. I had less than a handful of friends, and Tim was playing professional baseball in a city a few hours away. I was lonely and didn't have the mental or emotional capacity to strategize a new plan for my future; instead, I kept hoping and waiting for the next opportunity to present itself. Honestly, I felt like such a mess. On top of it all, Tim and I were planning a wedding . . . in South Africa.

For most of my teenage years and into early adulthood, I had only focused on the immediate "next thing" in my life. I had never considered life in the big picture. Being in no-man's-land can be discouraging because it leaves us anticipating an unknown future. When I think of my waiting season post–Miss Universe, I think of the frustration, anxiety, loneliness, and feelings of hopelessness I struggled with because I didn't feel I was making significant progress in any area of my life.

On the work front, I received a no more often than a yes. When I did get a yes, I often felt those opportunities would have required me to compromise. I constantly questioned the purpose of my life. I felt so stuck. I searched Pinterest for quotes on self-confidence and self-belief. I made a vision board. I tried coming up with a plan. Nothing worked because my self-confidence was running on empty. Looking back, I want to give this younger version of Demi a hug and remind her that Jesus doesn't ask us to strive for success or fame. He doesn't expect us to have every aspect of our lives perfectly sorted out. He simply asks us to follow Him.

During this period, I was invited to be a guest on several podcasts. The questions I got asked the most were, "What's next for Demi-Leigh" or "What big project are you working on?" I'd silently respond, *I'm doing my best. Mind your own business, Patricia*. Phew! But seriously, I couldn't face being asked that question on a podcast or on an Instagram Live knowing hundreds or even thousands of people would be listening. I had no idea what to tell all those people. And if I admitted the truth ("Uh, I'm not sure."), I was afraid I'd come off like a giant disappointment.

So I dodged talking about my future altogether. In fact, I came up with the brilliant plan of respectfully turning down all those opportunities. For example, I opened a second email account and pretended to be my own assistant. Why? Because I wanted to avoid people having direct access to me so that they couldn't throw more questions my way that I knew I couldn't answer. I would respond with something like, "Good day! Thank you for your request. Demi is not currently accepting new opportunities. We would love to stay in touch and reconsider at a future date when her schedule frees up. Warmest regards." Did I sign off with a name? Absolutely not! I couldn't get myself to fabricate *that* big of a lie!

Although at the time I viewed waiting as failure, looking back, it was a period of preparation. I know what you may be thinking: *It's so hard to grasp these truths when you're in the thick of waiting.* I get it. It took years to rebuild my confidence and to finally see a clearer future.

WAITING CAN SEEM LIKE WASTING

Compared to previous centuries, our generation is the first to grow up with technology that gives us instant gratification: email, social media, apps to ease every task, speed dating, Netflix, same-day delivery, fast food, fast *everything*. Instant gratification also leads to the release of more dopamine in our brains, which can become addictive. Unfortunately, two of the most important things in life do not develop fast: character and relationships. And these are the only two things we take with us when we leave earth. God is concerned with the not-so-fast things, which often clashes with our myopic perspective and need for instant gratification. God doesn't need fast *anything*, but we have become addicted to fast *everything*.

When we pinpoint the root of why waiting sucks, it may come down to the fact that we are selfish beings who want things done our way. In our time. Right now. Ask me how I know? Instead of trusting God's plan, I fabricated a lie of being my own assistant for a while. Instead of focusing on serving Him, I was fixated on making my next career move. During my waiting seasons, I have caught myself many times *playing* God instead of *trusting* God and *serving* God.

In those moments of waiting, we might feel like nothing good happens, or that *now* is better. Waiting can seem like wasting time, but I have learned that there is a flip side to a waiting season.

BENEFITS TO WAITING

Depending on the situation and our mindset, waiting can evoke polar emotions in us, ranging from patience one day to impatience the next, excitement one morning to anxiety the next. However, there can be spiritual and psychological benefits associated with waiting.

Seeing Your Life from God's Perspective

I walked outside one afternoon to take a picture of the beautiful sunset reflecting in our pool. I thought getting closer to the pool would give me a better view, but as I got closer, the pretty picture disappeared. I realized that I had to take a few steps back to see the full picture.

It works the same way in life. Having a close-up view or being caught in the situation can give us tunnel vision, but creating some physical distance or distance through time to actively seek the full picture, God's picture, can often lead us to seeing and understanding *better.* When I was living in New York and navigating the concrete jungle post–Miss Universe, there was seldom time to look up and enjoy the view, or the skyscrapers in this case. I was focused on hustling and paying the rent for my fifth-floor walk-up apartment, so journaling about understanding that there is a perfect plan for my future felt so far-fetched and impractical in that moment.

Learning to Make Better Decisions

Instead of chasing after the passions God had planted in my heart and cultivating a community that could help guide me and pray for me, I was chasing followers, attending the "right" events, and wearing the designer outfits to win approval from the fashion police. I remember feeling so stressed going to modeling castings with an outdated designer bag, thinking it wouldn't impress the casting agent.

These days, Tim and I have a process of pausing, praying, and then seeking wisdom from trusted advisors before making any decisions that impact our lives. We won't make our final decision until we have actively read God's Word, prayed, and spoken to every advisor and weighed everyone's opinions. We never derail from this decision-making process no matter how much pressure we are under. Gathering wisdom can certainly put things on hold, but it gives you time to evaluate what you're hoping for and consider possible outcomes. It also gives you time to gather more information and adjust expectations where needed. Once you've had time to gather the necessary facts and wise opinions, you can rely on discernment rather than fear or panic.

Practicing Patience and Mindfulness

After handing over the Miss Universe title and declining all those podcast and interview requests via my pretend assistant, I later realized that being vulnerable and honest is more important, meaningful, and relatable to people than having a perfectly put-together story to tell. Because guess what? Most of us are in the same uncertain boat. If you feel alone in your imperfect story like I did post–Miss Universe, please don't. We are all just secretly trying to figure out our next best move.

Developing an Eternal Mindset

Life on earth is temporary, but as believers, our ultimate hope lies in eternity with God. Having this mindset helps us endure uncertainty and setbacks with greater resilience. God works in all situations, even in the waiting. He brings about clarity, growth, and alignment with His perfect plan. We know there is an Enemy who comes to steal, kill, and destroy. But Jesus has come so that we can have life abundantly (John 10:10).

The apostle Paul understood this reality when he wrote to the church in Rome: "We ourselves, who have the firstfruits of the Spirit, groan inwardly as we wait eagerly for adoption as sons, the redemption of our bodies. For in this hope we were saved" (Romans 8:23–24 ESV). On this side of heaven we'll experience "inward groans"—the deep, internal longings that are sometimes hard to put into words. It's that profound ache when confronting trauma and pain and the questions we don't have the answers to. It's the agony of losing a loved one or seeing a parent endure the horrors of chemotherapy and watching their skin cling to their bones from all the weight loss. It's the mental pain you endure when you walk up five flights of stairs because you couldn't afford living in a building with an elevator. And with every step you climb, your confidence slips away because you don't know where your next paycheck is coming from. It's the longing for a world free from injustices and human suffering. These inward groans are reflective of a spiritual longing, a longing for the ultimate fulfillment of God's promises.

With an eternal mindset, "we wait eagerly" for final restoration where all things are made new. But there's not just hope for the future; there's hope now! The hope of heaven is not just one day; as believers, it's *today*! Throughout Jesus' ministry, He continuously shared that the kingdom had arrived. He taught us to pray, "Thy kingdom come, Thy will be done in earth, as it is in heaven" (Matthew 6:10 KJV). We don't have to live our lives waiting until we die to experience wholeness; instead, it's accessible to us here and now through Christ. We're not like survivors stranded on earth, waiting for rescue. Jesus came to be the answer to our waiting, offering immediate hope even as we anticipate joining Him on the redeemed earth one day.

WAITING, GOD'S WAY

The Bible is filled with stories of waiting and redemption, from Abraham and Sarah waiting for a child to the Israelites waiting to reach the promised land. These stories have encouraged me during seasons of waiting. When we read the stories in the Bible, let's not forget that they are Bible realities. They are based on real people who lived thousands of years ago, whose life stories God still uses to show us how we are supposed to live our lives. One of the best examples in the Bible of someone waiting God's way is found in the book of Ruth.

Only two books in the Old Testament receive their names from women: Ruth and Esther. You go, girls! The name *Ruth* most likely comes from a Moabite/Hebrew word meaning "friendship," which foreshadows the book's storyline![1] Although Ruth was not born an Israelite, God used her to greatly influence the nation of Israel. If you aren't familiar with this story, let me give you a quick lesson.

Due to a famine, Naomi (who was an Israelite); her husband, Elimelech; and their two sons left Bethlehem and relocated to Moab. Over a ten-year period, Naomi's husband and both sons died, leaving her with her Moabite daughters-in-law, Ruth and Orpah (Ruth 1:1–5). Hearing that the famine was over, Naomi decided to return to her people in Bethlehem, accepting the fact that she would be alone and probably forgotten for the remainder of her life (1:12–13). While on the road back to Bethlehem, Naomi told her daughters-in-law multiple times to remain in Moab and not come with her (1:11–15). But Ruth refused.

She would not abandon Naomi in such challenging times to fight for herself. She assured her mother-in-law, "Don't urge me to leave you or to turn back from you. Where you go I will go, and where you stay I will stay. Your people will be my people and your God my God" (1:16).

Ruth continued with Naomi toward Bethlehem, which was a sixty-to-seventy-five-mile trip and probably took around seven to ten days! While accompanying Naomi back to Bethlehem, Ruth vowed to "pick up the leftover grain behind anyone in whose eyes I find favor" (2:2) to provide for both her and Naomi. Can you imagine having just lost your husband, but you press on to care for your mother-in-law by leaving everyone and everything you know behind and moving to a strange land?

Ruth probably didn't know a soul in Naomi's hometown of Bethlehem, but it didn't stop her. Instead of sitting around waiting for God to bring friends or a new spouse, she got up, went to a barley field, and collected scraps to provide for her and Naomi. While doing so, she caught the attention of a man named Boaz. It wasn't Ruth's looks that caught Boaz's attention. Boaz had been told all about what Ruth had done for her mother-in-law since the death of her husband. How she had left her family and her homeland to come and live with people she did not know (2:11).

To make a long story short, because of Ruth's character, loyalty, and obedience, Boaz eventually married her. This was significant because Ruth went on to become the great-grandmother of King David (4:17) as well as part of Jesus' lineage too! All because Ruth was *willing* to take action, to be obedient, and to get uncomfortable. She refused to sit around while she waited for what was next. At the beginning of the story, Ruth and Naomi were in a tragic state, but at the end both were singing praises. Even the other women in Bethlehem proclaimed that Ruth was better for Naomi than seven sons (4:15).[2]

BE WILLING AND WORK THROUGH THE WAIT

Ruth's story teaches us that as we're waiting, God is working. At the same time, waiting is not an excuse to get comfortable or avoid responsibilities. Ruth is such a great example of working through the waiting. She turned her waiting season into a willing season. Her story has inspired me to be willing through stagnant seasons to keep trusting God to use me where I am with what I've got. Following my Miss Universe year, I found myself in the back of casting lines with the newbies—like I was starting all over again. I couldn't book opportunities for runway shows, but I was able to get the smaller jobs where lead makeup artists used me as a canvas to demonstrate the makeup look for other backstage artists to replicate. Even though I didn't get the jobs I hoped for, it gave me an opportunity to bring a little calmness and kindness into a chaotic backstage environment by sharing a tiny glimpse of God's love through conversation and serving.

To be willing or having a sense of willingness simply means "to be ready, eager, or prepared to do something."[3] A willing person is not opposed to act, rather she strives to work with energy, care, and intentionality. It's the opposite of being resistant, reluctant, or resentful. Being willing implies a proactive mindset, whether it's undertaking a task, embracing change, or facing challenges with a positive attitude. Willingness embodies the essence of true faith: moving forward with confidence despite the timeline. Jesus' life is our most profound example of this.

When Jesus turned water to wine in John 2, He said, "My hour has not yet come" (v. 4 ESV). This phrase is repeated throughout the Gospel of John, referring to Jesus' future crucifixion and glorification. He knew He had to wait for the Father's perfect timing to endure the cross and pay the penalty for our sin. He acknowledged His hour would come, but until it did, Jesus was *ready*, *eager*, and *prepared* to show the Father's love to the world. As I reflect on Jesus' waiting season, here are a few things He modeled that we could implement in our lives:

Find friends to do life with.

Jesus didn't do life alone. He specifically chose twelve dudes to be part of His close friend group. They traveled together, they served together, they ate together, they stayed up all night and shared who they were crushing on! (Okay, maybe not that last one!) But what we see in the lives of Jesus and Ruth—His great-great-great-great-(a bunch more *greats*) grandmother—are deep friendships. In one of Harvard's longest-standing studies ever conducted, researchers wanted to know what was responsible for health and happiness throughout a person's life. Can you guess what the predicator was? *More money?* No. *Bigger house?* No. Of the people surveyed, those who were *most satisfied in their relationships* were the healthiest and happiest.[4]

I totally relate to this. One of my unhappiest times coincided with one of my loneliest times. I often found myself sitting alone in my NYC apartment, days passing without anyone to talk to in person or to cook dinner with. The brightest moments were phone conversations with Tim, who was juggling a crazy baseball schedule, and the sweet interactions with strangers, who sometimes kindly opened my building door for me after I'd forced myself to step out for a coffee. I knew my only source of connection couldn't come from a phone call with my long-distance fiancé, but I struggled with forging meaningful relationships in a new country and culture. Truthfully, my past Miss Universe title and my fiancé's presence in the public eye made me doubt everyone's intentions.

Psychiatrist Robert J. Waldinger said, "Loneliness kills. It's as powerful as smoking or alcoholism."[5] The point is, we need to be willing to surround ourselves with good people. Maybe you already have a solid friend circle. If that's the case, go deeper. Serve, eat, laugh, and cry together. If you're struggling to find or make friends, keep putting yourself in situations to connect.

Create time to be *alone* with God.

After Jesus fed the five thousand, He "dismissed the crowds" and "went up on the mountain by himself to pray" (Matthew 14:23

ESV). This was a regular habit of His. He knew that in order to pour into other people, He needed to be filled up!

During my post–Miss Universe era, I convinced myself that I was supposed to spend every minute working to discover my next big thing. There was no time to have fun or to spend on self-reflection. Spending time in God's Word also took a back seat. What a pot of bad self-made advice. Spending time with Jesus is not a chore or a burden; it's meant to be an encounter where we get to deepen our intimacy with God. Find a time that works for you and use the time to journal, pray for someone or something, read a Bible passage, write out your observations from Scripture, sing a song, create a song, meditate on a psalm, write a poem, or paint.

Be willing to be interruptible.

While Jesus was traveling, a woman who had been suffering from a chronic issue for twelve years approached Him in a large crowd. The woman courageously reached out and touched Jesus' garment. Immediately He sensed that power had gone out from Him, and He stopped to inquire who touched Him. Despite being in a hurry to attend to another pressing matter (the healing of Jairus's daughter), Jesus took the time to address this woman's needs (Mark 5:25–34). He was a pretty busy guy but still allowed Himself to be interruptible. Whether in the grocery store, gas station, or on a walk with your kids, keep an eye out for those who are hurting. Don't get too busy. Be willing to love others. You never know the positive effects your goodness can do. The effects of your compassion will branch out from one simple act of brotherly love. I wish I had been more willing to love others in my post–Miss Universe era instead of only focusing on my own hurdles and heartaches. Loving others would have helped me to see beyond the moment I felt stuck in.

Create a plan.

To make the Last Supper happen, Jesus created a plan. He selected a location, gave instructions to prepare a meal, arranged for the meal to be held in private, then created a guest list (Luke 22). Without making the proper arrangements ahead of time, maybe it would have been called the Last Snack! Although this is an oversimplistic example, while Jesus was still waiting to go to the cross, He was willing to plan. As the popular saying goes, "If you *fail to plan* then you *plan to fail.*" A plan without a purpose is just a to-do list. I failed in figuring out my purpose as a part of my plan. Make sure you include the purpose behind your plan, and don't stop until your goals are specific and detailed.

Serve someone.

In John 13, Jesus did the unthinkable: He washed the feet of His friends. In the culture of that time, foot washing was typically performed by the lowest servants and was considered a menial task. By taking on this role Himself, Jesus was breaking down social and cultural barriers to emphasize the importance of serving others. It was a powerful demonstration of humility and servitude. He was teaching His disciples that leadership in His kingdom is characterized by humble service, not positions of power or authority. The application is simple: find a way to serve and be helpful. During my off days as Miss Universe (which were very few), I enjoyed volunteering at a local soup kitchen in New York City. I was surrounded by other like-minded people who gave of their precious time to serve others. I showed up with the intention to love on others but started realizing that my cup got filled too.

As you can see from Jesus' life, being willing really sets you up to do life with people, experience divine God moments, and leave a lasting footprint. When I stopped waiting and started being willing, I was able to open my hands and ask God every single day to show me His way. Let's be real though. The feeling of hopelessness didn't disappear overnight. I didn't figure out my five- or ten-year plan right away, but with the help of mentors who guided me in discerning God's will, I can confidently say that I believe things are always "figureoutable." If you feel stuck, I encourage you to try something wild and freeing, trusting God instead of playing God.

Staying willing and allowing God to use your struggles for His glory is the secret to turning your waiting season into your winning season. When life deals heavy blows, remember that in those moments the true victory comes from your courage to seek growth despite the enormous amount of grief you're experiencing. Victory in those waiting situations could mean getting out of bed regardless of the headache and heartache you're experiencing. Victory might also mean being vulnerable and recognizing that you're not able to win on your own right now. Asking for help does not equal weakness.

GOD-WINK MOMENTS THAT KEEP YOU GOING

Waiting can hurt or remind you that you're lost, but when you surrender the process to God, He will show up for you in ways you can never imagine, ways so personal to you that you can't help but feel loved, seen, and cared for. Shortly after I handed over my title as Miss Universe in December 2018, I was approached to be part of filming an exciting project in South America. I was thrilled for many reasons, but mainly because I was still searching for my next big thing. Two weeks before filming, though, the project got postponed indefinitely due to weather complications. I was sad as the project was as good as "canceled" until further notice.

The cancellation meant that a whole month freed up in my schedule. So instead of traveling to South America, I unexpectedly got to go back home to South Africa to visit my family. My sister Franje's thirteenth birthday was a few days after I landed in Johannesburg. It was a sweet surprise to spend that special day with her. My stepmom had a tradition of getting my sister cupcakes on her birthday, mainly for our friends and family to enjoy since my sister was fed through a gastrostomy tube due to her inability to effectively swallow food as a result of her cerebellar agenesis diagnosis. A big cake always went to waste, and cupcakes were a fun alternative. We had a great day celebrating Franje with friends and family we didn't see often. It was like a mini reunion. Pappa Bennie pulled out the braai (the South African version of a barbeque, but better). And both the *oumas* (grandmothers) prepared the sides. We sang happy birthday, blew out birthday candles, and had the best party.

We had no idea it would be Franje's last birthday celebration on earth. She would pass away just over two months later from lifelong complications as a result of her being born with a brain dysgenesis (disrupted brain development in utero). Even though at the time I thought I had missed out on a great work opportunity, nothing could have compared to the value of celebrating my sister's last earthly birthday with her. God showed up and gave me what I needed instead of what I wanted in the canceled job.

Fast-forward to a few weeks after Tim and I got married in 2020 when I received an unexpected call from my agent. "Demi, you won't believe it! Remember the project that got canceled last year? They want to know if you can start filming in three weeks!" I said yes and started packing. When we received the production schedule, I couldn't believe what I was reading. Our first day of filming would start on what would have been my sister's fourteenth birthday. I looked up at the sky and laughed. It was a total God-wink moment—when God is showing up backstage or on the sidelines or in the alley and whispering, "You go, girl! I've got you! Keep going." This was during a time in my life when I was constantly seeking God's presence and looking for His affirmation on my decisions. Although He didn't answer me in words, He gave me clear signs of His presence and His purpose for me.

On the first day of filming, also Franje's first heavenly birthday, I walked out of my hotel room to meet my agent in the restaurant for breakfast. I'd woken up that day sad about Franje yet excited about the first day of filming. I was a little skeptical about what the restaurant would offer since we were in a very remote area. *I should have brought more snacks*, I thought. I got in the line at the buffet, poured a big cup of coffee, and dished up some scrambled eggs and sausage. When I got to the end of the buffet, I saw what they were serving and nearly burst into tears.

God showed up for me in that dining hall like I could never have imagined. Right there in the corner, next to the fruit bowl, stood a stand of iced cupcakes. They weren't exactly like the kind my stepmom got for Franje's birthday, with big dollops of whipped cream cheese icing and decorated with the prettiest flowers or safari animals. In fact, they were dry and stale. But it was clear they were *cupcakes*! And you can bet I ate *two*! I felt like I was having my own little birthday party for my sister. The filming crew couldn't understand why I was eating two pieces of dry cake for breakfast. When I filled them in about my sister, multiple people got up, walked over to the buffet, got themselves a cupcake, and sat in solidarity with me to celebrate my sissy's first heavenly birthday. The cupcakes were so dry, we all dunked them in our coffee to make them more edible.

Through God's kindness, a very sad day turned into a very sweet story.

Through the chaos and moments of feeling alone, God never forgets us. With all the hurt in the world, He cared enough to comfort my aching heart in the sweetest way, and He cares for you too. I think God's kindness toward our smallest concerns speaks so much about His character. When your pain or unrelenting waiting feels irrelevant in the bigger scheme of things, it isn't irrelevant to Him. He cares for *all* His creation—the orchids and the weeds, the golden retrievers and the geese, the Nemos and the nurse sharks, the world and everything in it—but most of all, *you*!

Jesus expressed this to the crowds in His first ever recorded sermon by saying, "Look at the birds of the air; they do not sow or reap or store away in barns, and yet your heavenly Father feeds them. Are you not much more valuable than they?" (Matthew 6:26). In rhetorical fashion, *of course you are!* Of all that God created, we as human beings, divine image-bearers, are His most valuable creation. Cupcakes may seem small, but God cares about even the little things in our lives! Reflecting on God's kindness, David wrote, "How precious also are Your thoughts to me, O God! How vast is the sum of them! If I should count them, they would outnumber the sand" (Psalm 139:17–18 NASB1995). Speak that verse over yourself every day while standing in front of the bathroom mirror. I promise it'll put a smile on your face! God sees you as precious and valuable and has you on His mind always!

KNOW WHO YOU ARE WITH

Sometimes it's not about the waiting process itself as much as who we are waiting with. As if the moment at the breakfast buffet wasn't enough, God continued to show up and show off His thoughtfulness that day. As we wrapped up the first day of filming in South America, I walked to my trailer to change into comfortable clothes and slippers, pausing to look up and admire the stars. In the absence of city lights and pollution, the stars shone especially big and bright. They felt so near to the earth, like I could reach and touch them. The first constellation I noticed was the Southern Cross and its two pointers.

The Southern Cross consists of five individual stars that form a cross-like shape in the Southern Hemisphere's night sky. There are two bright stars to the left of the Southern Cross named Beta Centauri and Alpha Centauri, known as the "pointers" to the Southern Cross. They are very important for two main reasons.

Without the two pointers next to the Southern Cross, sky watchers cannot separate the true Southern Cross from several false crosses in the night sky.

Without the pointers, we would not be able to calculate the south celestial pole; therefore, we wouldn't be able to determine true south and know if we are on the right track.

Sixteenth-century European explorers used the Southern Cross as a navigation tool to quickly find due south (comparable to how the North Star is used for navigation in the Northern Hemisphere).[6] The Southern Cross has been a bright spot in the sky, offering assurance to many that they're going in the right direction. Since living in the United States, I don't ever get to see the Southern Cross because it never rises above the horizon in the Northern Hemisphere. If you're far enough south in Florida or Texas and are willing to stay up until the early morning hours, you might spot a glimpse of it in the right month of the year.[7] It holds a very special connection to me as it always reminds me of home. Noticing the Southern Cross while in South America was such a sweet surprise.

Seeing the Southern Cross served as a beautiful reminder that I don't have to worry about where I'm going if I know who I am going with. If you ever feel alone, forgotten, or uncertain about what step to take next, then pause and take a breath, search for the Pointer—the God of the whole universe—and ask Him to point you in the right direction. God works through the wait, even in the silence.

In most of our Bibles, going from the book of Malachi in the Old Testament to the book of Matthew in the New Testament is a simple flip of one page. But that page represents so much. Approximately four hundred years of waiting, to be exact. Scholars refer to this period (between the Old Testament and New Testament) as the "intertestamental period," also known as the "400 Silent Years." During this time, there were no recorded prophetic or divine messages, leading some to perceive it as a period of divine silence. However, beneath the surface, significant historical, cultural, and geopolitical events were shaping the world stage for the arrival of Jesus Christ and the start of the church.

Despite the perceived silence, God's providence was evident in several progressions: the establishment of the Roman empire, the building of roads and synagogues, Greek language, religious tolerance, the development of Jewish political parties, and more. All these things helped facilitate the timing of Jesus' birth, ministry, death, and resurrection, and the spread of the gospel. Though these four hundred years lacked explicit revelation, it was a time of profound preparation orchestrated by God.

This is a reminder that God doesn't operate on our timeline but on His. In Galatians 4:4, Paul proclaimed, "when the fullness of the time came, God sent His Son" (NASB). What Paul meant here is that when all the details of God's plan added up perfectly, He sent Jesus on a rescue mission. If I operated on my timeline and followed my plan, I would have missed out on a lot, including opportunities like saying happy birthday to my sister for the last time. We see our present, but God knows our future. In Jeremiah 29:11, although the nation of Israel would live in captivity and exile for seventy years due to their disobedience, God proclaimed, "For I know the plans I have for you . . . plans to prosper you and not to harm you, plans to give you hope and a future." Even in seasons of suffering and hardship, God has great plans for our lives.

And the next time you doubt it, consider writing this out and putting it up on your mirror, next to your computer, or on your fridge:

> During what might feel like a waiting season,
> be encouraged that no time is wasted.
> What feels like a no might be a "not now."
> What feels like a failure might be fickle feelings.
> And what feels like a period of silence might be
> your preparation period.
> God works through the wait.
> He's loud in the silence.
> Lean in.
> Look out for the God-winks.
> They'll keep you going.
> Most of all, stay willing through the waiting.

THREE

NOW YOU KNOW IN PART; THEN YOU'LL KNOW FULLY

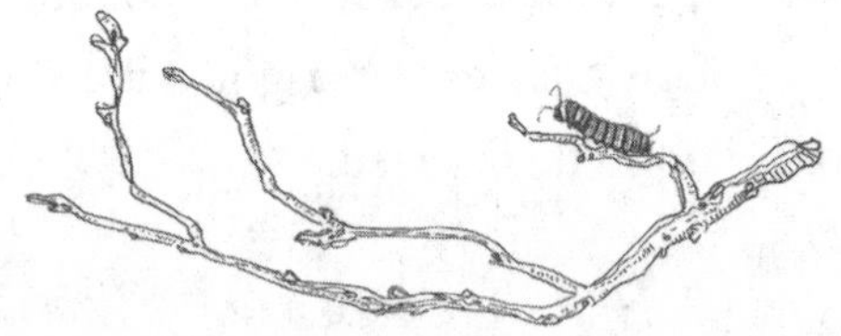

My friends had just finished singing "Happy Birthday" to me. I blew out the ten candles and was getting ready to cut the cake when the phone rang. The cake-cutting was paused as my mom jumped up and ran down the hallway to answer the phone. Eight middle school girls sat around a decorated table, mouths watering and calling dibs on the corner pieces with the most icing.

"Demi, it's for you!" my mom called from our home office. "Someone wants to wish you a happy birthday." As I walked toward her and wondered who'd be calling, I peeped over my shoulder to make sure no one claimed my piece.

"Happy birthday, Demi!" my stepmom, Elzabé, and my dad sang in unison on the other end of the line.

Dad apologized for calling so late but said he had a surprise.

"We want to send you a birthday gift on the fax line. Are you close to a fax right now?"

I started imagining what our family king of practical jokes could be sending me. "Yes! Of course!" I replied with a giggle. "Send away!"

If you don't know what a fax machine is or the noises it makes, you're missing out. After a few seconds of high and low decibel screeching, it would always swallow a piece of paper. Then, more ear-piercing shrieking. A few moments later, the machine would spit out the paper with the incoming message from the other end of the machine. It took about three minutes, which was a lifetime for me. When the noises stopped, the paper was still hot and the ink wet.

Turns out, none of my guesses were right, but my wildest dreams were about to come true. The fax read:

"Dems,"

. . .

"YOU"

. . .

"ARE"

. . .

"GOING"

. . .

"TO"

. . .

"BE"

. . .

"A BIG SISTER!"

"What is happening?" "Are you serious?" "A boy or a girl?" "Wait, seriously?" "When?" I rambled away while trying to make sense of the news. Even though I was extremely excited, I was also in shock. I had been an only child for ten years. What would the addition of a sibling look like? I'd always asked for a little brother or sister, and now that it was happening, it seemed surreal.

I started dreaming of the dress-up parties that my little sister and I would have. I calculated that by the time I turned eighteen and had a driver's license, she would be eight, and we could go shopping together. I'd also help her with homework and cheer her on at hockey or netball games, or whatever sport she chose to play, although I secretly hoped it would be field hockey because that was my favorite sport in school. I was ecstatic that I finally had someone to share things with that I didn't want to share with my parents. Like when the cute boy in class sent his friend to give me a heart-shaped letter he wrote because he was too shy to do it himself. Finally, I would have someone in my corner who would understand me, a forever friend.

When I think of the phrase "big sister," a few words come to mind: *brave, caring, fierce, protective, wise.* In my mind a big sister figure is someone who serves as a role model to her siblings or younger friends. She loves deeply, protects fiercely, and fights bravely for those who view her as a big sister. She is someone who cares enough to be honest and transparent with those she loves to protect. Her life experience offers her wisdom that her younger siblings or peers still must gain. Out of love, she shares that wisdom freely. That was the responsibility I was about to take on as a big sister. I promised myself that I was going to be the best big sister and that my little sister would have someone she could lean on and look up to.

The months waiting to meet her were long and tedious. The excitement was greater than looking forward to a dream vacation you booked a year ago. The anticipation was stronger than waiting to finish high school and move into your dorm room after getting the news that you were accepted into your favorite university. And no trip to the mall was ever the same. I started noticing matching shirts or bags for siblings and wanted to buy them all. Time moved slowly. Finally, we got a call on February 27, 2006, a few days before we expected her arrival. I was officially a big sister! Franje was born right in the middle of my exam week, so I had to finish my exams before I could fly to meet her, which was torture.

Because my parents had divorced when I was very young, I was used to traveling alone across the country multiple times a year to visit my dad. But this visit was going to be different. I remember stepping onto the airplane with an "unaccompanied minor" sign around my neck. I had packed a little gift for my sister that I'd bought with my own money. I kept it in my carry-on to make sure it would get to her safely. My dad picked me up from the airport, and the two-hour drive home through traffic was painful. We finally pulled into the driveway, and I jumped out of the car, leaving my bags in the trunk to deal with later. My dad quietly unlocked the front door and we walked down the hallway on our tippy-toes in case Franje was sleeping. She was, so we gently knocked on the bedroom door.

"Come in," my stepmom whispered. I froze as the door creaked. I was so scared to wake this little baby. My stepmom was sitting on the bed, holding my little sister in her arms as she slept. I remember she was wearing the daintiest newborn dress and I thought that she was even prettier than any of the baby dolls I had ever seen. "Hi, Dems! Come and meet your sister." My stepmom smiled at me. "Would you like to hold her?" *I do, but I don't know how,* I thought. I was so scared that I would break her! She was four weeks old when we met for the first time. I spent that school vacation in the small town of Potchefstroom changing a diaper for the first time, learning how to ensure the bathwater was the perfect temperature for a newborn, and feeding a baby a bottle. We had long conversations, Franje and I, because I was convinced that she understood every word, even though she could not respond. After all, we had *a lot* to catch up on.

A few weeks later we were sitting around the kitchen table eating brunch, and I could sense that my dad was distracted. He and Elzabé had just returned from a routine six-week newborn checkup. He mentioned that they had found some concerning factors about Franje. She wasn't gaining enough weight, and they'd found that her head wasn't growing in proportion to what was expected for a baby her age. I was concerned but didn't pay it too much attention. *She is a baby, and they grow so fast, right?* I remember thinking, *There's great technology these days. I'm sure it will all be fine. Let's just give it time.*

Weeks and weeks went by where there were no improvements with Franje, yet they were unable to find a diagnosis. I went home, but my dad and Elzabé scheduled doctor visit after doctor visit, specialist after specialist. At four months, Franje was finally diagnosed with a brain dysgenesis—which means that the normal development of the white and gray matter of the brain had been disrupted. The result was threefold: a subtotal cerebellar agenesis, an underdeveloped corpus callosum and brain stem, as well as microcephaly.

A subtotal cerebellar agenesis is a near-total lack of a cerebellum. In simpler terms, the cerebellum is one of three parts of the brain, and while small, it's pretty important. The cerebellum is responsible for muscle control (think things like balance and movement), and it also plays a role in other brain functions, like language processing and memory. In other words, living without it would be very difficult. Franje probably had about 10 percent of a normal cerebellum, and the rest of her brain, inclusive of white and gray matter, didn't develop normally either. According to the National Organization for Rare Disorders, "The exact incidence and prevalence of the disorder in the general population is unknown. Congenital isolated cerebellar agenesis is considered an extremely rare occurrence."[1] So that means children born without a cerebellum can present on a continuum ranging from normal functionality to severely disabled. In Franje's case, she presented as severely disabled. To this day, her diagnosis still breaks my heart.

WHEN YOU FEEL TOTALLY ALONE

Franje's condition was never identified by any of the prenatal tests, so her diagnosis came as a complete shock to our family. It felt like one of those moments where there is a fork in the road and your GPS loses its signal, leaving you hoping that you picked the right way home. Because of the limited research available on her condition, there was no guidance on what the future would look like. It was all a big guess. We got polarizing opinions. Some children with Franje's same condition were functioning at a near-normal level of development; other children had been functioning at the level of a baby their whole life.

Have you ever aced a job interview, received great feedback from your new potential boss, even had the conversation about relocating, only to end up not getting the job and being left without any logical explanation as to why? The disappointment of unmet expectations can feel like a real loss. Unmet expectations are the loss of something we never experienced in the first place. Think of the dating situation that doesn't work out when you thought he was the one. Or the time you were praying for years for a healthy baby only to receive a negative pregnancy test yet again. When we add a high value to an expectation, our minds and bodies can't distinguish between an actual loss and an expectation that was not met and therefore process the unmet expectations as a real loss.[2]

The year I turned eleven, I tried to stay positive and hopeful and prayed every night that God would heal my sister, but the more we learned about her diagnosis, the harder it was to accept the facts. Learning about her condition shattered all my dreams about our shopping days, homework sessions, and all the other sisterly things Franje and I would never get to do together. The way I dealt with this situation as a child was by stepping up as a big sister and doing my best not to cause any additional work for my parents. I stuck to my corner, did my own thing, and never really asked for help. I became independent, figuring out problems on my own. I didn't become distant; I just became reserved. I thought it best not to share unnecessary details about my life with my parents. I didn't want to add more work to their already full plate. To be clear, this was an expectation I planted on myself. This was never an expectation from my parents.

But it meant I felt deeply alone. Although I was surrounded by loved ones, I decided to carry the weight of meeting all my own needs, so it was hard to understand that God was always there for me to depend on. When you spend a lot of time on your own, it feels like being adrift in the deep, dark depths of the ocean, and it's hard to see that you're not actually alone. Even if the reality is that God is equipping you, it doesn't always feel that way.

WHEN YOUR PRAYERS GO UNANSWERED

Franje made very slow developmental progress, but every small step in the right direction was a big win. With the help of physical therapy and neurological development programs, we started seeing a glimmer of hope! At age one, Franje started doing movements that were similar to crawling. She also seemed to express excitement when she recognized certain voices. We accepted that Franje would never be able to function at the same level as her peers, not unless there was a miracle, but these new signs gave us so much hope that she might be able to have a chance of living without being 100 percent dependent on others for survival.

But that glimmer of hope soon turned into a pit of darkness when she developed West syndrome at one year of age. Following intensive treatment, the condition went into remission. However, a year later the condition returned, wiping out all the previous developmental progress she'd been making. Although she survived, she never recuperated, and the setback left her functioning at the level of a three-month-old baby for the rest of her life. All memory and motor skills she had learned in the two years prior vanished. Her ability to start crawling or hold her own bottle disappeared like it was all a dream. She had seizures that left her and everyone present exhausted and emotionally drained. It was awful to see her endure such pain and not be able to do anything to stop it. The fact that there was such limited research on Franje's diagnosis at the time, specifically in South Africa, left my parents having to navigate a trial-and-error process. Years of this went by. Weekly emergency room hospital visits were the norm.

Franje needed to have full-time care as she was fully dependent on us for survival. My parents were sleep-deprived for years. Anyone who loves someone with a traumatic diagnosis knows how this story feels. You know what it's like to barely have time for your partner or your other kids. You know what it's like to take turns sleeping in the guest bedroom to give your partner a chance to sleep while the other person watches over your loved one. You know what it's like to balance the job you need for the insurance and the income with caregiving. You know what it's like for work or the wildly rare night off to be interrupted by urgent medical phone calls. You know what it's like for family holidays, trips, school concerts, or meals to get canceled at the last second for an emergency trip to the hospital instead.

We have a small family, and Franje's care truly came down to the three of us. Over the next decade, as much as I learned about the complex medical care of my vulnerable sister, I also learned how to shut down my own emotions inside a hard and brittle shell. I developed thick skin and learned never to show when I was hurting, sad, mad, or disappointed. Instead of feeling or being, I learned to *do*. *Doing* became my default setting. It still is.

Rather than process internally first, I jump into action and do what needs to be done. But when the chaos calms and the dust settles, I collapse. When the pressure ceases, I'm depleted, burned out, empty, and questioning who I am. Placing my identity in the immediate situation or opportunity in front of me is a trap I recognize and manage more proactively now. Setting boundaries for myself, knowing what my traps are, and proactively identifying them has helped me not to ignore my emotions but to navigate them in a healthier way.

As the years passed and Franje became more ill, my childlike hope vanished. I became frustrated because I couldn't understand the purpose of all she had to endure. As a sixteen-year-old, I was frustrated at all the unanswered prayers I had prayed. I also had many questions that went unanswered.

Why won't God heal her when I know He can?

Why did He allow this to happen to Franje?

Why do innocent people and children suffer?

Why do my parents have to see their daughter hurting?

Why does this feel so hopeless?

Why?

Why?

Why?

My faith was rattled throughout my teenage years into my early adulthood. The unanswered questions made me question God's kindness. I couldn't comprehend the purpose of all this pain and torment, and I felt so far away from God. He felt like an acquaintance instead of a friend. The only comfort I was able to hold on to was God's track record in other people's lives.

At the time, I highly doubted if God's grace would count for our family. I highly doubted if He would show goodness and kindness to our family like He did throughout the Bible. I allowed the Enemy to do his job by creating doubt around God's character. There was a time I felt like I only believed in Jesus because it felt like the right thing to do. Then my dad looked at me one day and said, "Demi, I don't know what the purpose of all this is. Why do we believe in a God who allows an innocent child to suffer like this?" My stepmom's dream was to visit the homeland: Israel. And because of the ongoing years of turmoil in the Middle East, my dad agreed to accompany her purely because he loved her, not because he was interested in Jesus at that point. His experience on that trip taught me that the Lord uses what's important to us to remind us that He is near.

My dad is a visual person. If he can't see it, he struggles to believe it. When he got back from Israel—where he had touched Jesus' empty tomb, walked past the same olive trees Jesus did in the garden of Gethsemane, and dipped his hand in the same waters Jesus walked on in the sea of Galilee—his hardened heart finally warmed back up to God's unchanging, ever-powerful, promise-keeping character. He was so impacted when he saw the Bible come to life with his own eyes. For the first time, my dad believed without putting contingencies on God.

My own breakthrough was influenced by my dad's change of heart. I eventually realized that I could live the rest of my life either questioning God's plan or trusting God's plan. I don't think we will know the complete impact Franje's life had until we meet again in heaven, but I do believe that it is significant. In the meantime, God used what is important to me—food, the Southern Cross, and my family—to remind me of His nearness and sweetness through it all.

40 SECONDS OF COMPASSION

I was in Reno, Nevada, judging the Miss USA pageant in May 2019 when my dad called to tell me that Franje was not doing great and was back in the hospital. He kept me updated throughout the week. On the morning I was scheduled to fly back to New York, he called to say her condition was critical. I frantically checked all the flights to see if I could make it back to South Africa. But with the significant time zone difference and Reno not being the most accessible place to fly out from, I missed all the flights to South Africa that day. It took three flights to get me back to New York, and none of them had Wi-Fi for me to check in with my dad. Every time I had a layover, I would immediately call my dad when we touched down to see how Franje was doing, just to hear, "Dems, she's not great."

Sitting on the plane at the other end of the world, knowing that I might miss my chance to say goodbye to my sister while trying to hold it together was brutal. I felt guilty and helpless. There was absolutely no way for me to get to South Africa until at least two days later with the sixteen hours of flight time and time zone difference. I woke up the next morning in New York to the saddest news I'd ever received. I missed my opportunity to send my little sister off to heaven. Franje passed away on May 4, 2019, after her body fought its final battle.

It's been years, and I'm still processing what I learned from being Franje's sister. But at her core, my sister taught me that when we look at all human beings through God's lens, we will know that everyone is an image-bearer of God. When we look at imperfect people through the lens of a perfect Creator, we get to see people for who they were created to be. Scripture is clear that we were created in love, by love, and for love. When we can acknowledge the love with which a person was created by their heavenly Father, we will be able to view them through a lens of love and compassion. One of the greatest ways God has shown me compassion was when He went before me and set me up to celebrate one last birthday with Franje.

The word *compassion* originates from a twelfth-century Latin word meaning to "suffer with" someone. It's not just understanding the way someone feels but choosing to share in their affliction. According to a Harvard medical study, 56 percent of physicians feel that they don't have time to be empathetic with their patients.[3] Medical researchers Dr. Stephen Trzeciak and Dr. Anthony Mazzarelli, who were likely as stunned as you and me to hear that doctors don't have time to empathize, followed up with their own study: "How long *does* it actually take for a meaningful expression of compassion to happen?" They investigated work from Johns Hopkins University where researchers asked physicians to conduct random interviews with breast cancer patients. The oncologist would read from a script to determine if it would reduce patient anxiety. Here is an example of what they said:

"I know this has been a tough experience to go through, and I want you to know that I am here with you. . . . We are here together, and we will go through this together. . . . I will be with you each step along the way."[4]

This "script" took roughly forty seconds to recite! That's it. And just forty seconds of genuine care and compassion from the oncologist saw a statistically relevant decrease in cancer patient anxiety! Showing compassion isn't just talk; it has meaningful impact! Our family felt this firsthand when bad news was shared in the absence of compassion. One of the neurologists who initially diagnosed Franje broke the news by telling my parents, "Your daughter will never walk, so circle back in a few years and get a funky wheelchair for her." The doctor's insensitivity was louder than these words. It would've taken less than forty seconds for him to have said, "I am so sorry to have to share the news of your daughter's diagnosis. Let me assure you that our faculty will be here every step of the way to guide you to the best of our ability as you care for Franje."

Do you have forty seconds today to be intentional with someone who is hurting or who just needs some love? Perhaps you could compliment the barista at your local coffee shop for making a great cup of coffee. Send a text to follow up on the hard situation a friend is walking through. Perhaps help someone fold up their stroller before boarding a plane, or give the sweet boy with Down syndrome a high five and tell him he is awesome. One of the most significant moments of my life was when the man who would become my husband reached out with that kind of compassion for me and my sister.

At the time, I was unaware of who Tim Tebow was. American sports are not a thing in South Africa. So when I received a message from this guy who was inviting my sister to his foundation's *Night to Shine*, I was skeptical. I had never heard of these unique events designed to celebrate people like my little sister. Unbeknownst to me, Tim had heard an interview I gave about Franje, sharing the story of how she was born with severe special needs. I spoke of how our family had been alienated by our community, our church, and even our friends. During thirteen years of suffering, and with countless hospital admissions, my parents received only two visits from the pastors from the congregation they were members of at that time. Friendships often disappeared into thin air. I wanted to believe that it wasn't because people didn't care and more so that they didn't know how to handle the situation and therefore defaulted to doing nothing. So reading Tim's email and hearing about his organization felt surreal to me. The fact that there was a community that chose to celebrate people around the world who are so often seen as the least, the last, or the lost resonated with a deep loneliness I had carried for years.

The Tim Tebow Foundation (TTF) has worked very closely with the disability community for years, and *Night to Shine* is an initiative started in 2015. A worldwide prom for people with special needs and disabilities, it is a night when the red carpet is rolled out, shoes get shined, cameras flash, and crowds gather to cheer and celebrate each honored guest in attendance. At the end of the evening, *every single guest* gets crowned as the king or the queen of the prom. The crowning is an integral part of *Night to Shine* as the hope is for every attendee to know that they are worthy of love and extremely valued, not just by society but by the King of the universe because they are His royalty. The year Tim heard my interview about Franje, they were hosting a *Night to Shine* in South Africa for the first time. After enduring years of painful loss of friends and community, I was blessed that Tim took forty seconds to reach out and invite Franje.

Looking back, I chuckle now because if you know Tim, you'll know that he is not the email type of guy. But he patiently and kindly responded to all my follow-up questions and offered to set up a phone call to discuss the event further. That call was only meant to be about five or ten minutes, but God had other plans. When I eventually hung up, I looked at my call log and realized that we'd been speaking for two hours, twenty-four minutes, and six seconds! *Did I just meet my husband?* I thought. Spoiler alert: since that first phone call, not a day has gone by that Tim and I have not spoken.

Due to Franje's medical condition and fragility, she was never able to attend *Night to Shine*, but you better believe she got her crown and was named the queen of our hearts. My little sister introduced me to my husband, so she gets full credit as our little matchmaker!

When Tim and I first met, we didn't have a ton in common, but we had so much *in purpose*. Getting to live out our purpose of loving God and loving people as a married couple has molded the foundation of our relationship. While God was laying the foundation of what would become one of my life's greatest purposes—fighting for hurting people—He had already set Tim's heart on fire for the very same thing. While I still may not fully understand why my little sister was born with a severe disability (believe me, it's one of the first questions I'll ask God when I meet Him face-to-face one day), I can at least look back and see God's hand in and throughout it all. When tragedy strikes, it's understandable to ask God why. Why demands understanding. Over the years, though, I've been challenged to not ask God *why* but to ask *where*. "Where are You working in my suffering?" *Where* sets God's presence above our own understanding and closure. As hard as this is, when we ask God *where* instead of *why*, we are choosing to trust His goodness and greatness.

There may be painful circumstances in your life that don't make sense now, but know that one day they will. God's trustworthy hand in it all is undeniable. The very first Christians had similar questions about their suffering. And the apostle Paul offered them this explanation in his letter to the church in Corinth: "For now we see in a mirror dimly, but then face to face. Now I know in part; then I shall know fully, even as I have been fully known" (1 Corinthians 13:12 ESV). What Paul was likely referring to were the lower quality brass and bronze mirrors of that day that were commonly used in the city of Corinth, Greece.[5] Ancient handheld mirrors showed distorted or incomplete reflections, so Paul drew a parallel to our own limited understanding of life and God.

In essence, he was saying that our perception of the world and our experience of it is like looking through a distorted lens. Imagine looking at your reflection in a foggy mirror from all the shower steam. We don't have a complete view of everything, but God does. We may not get all the answers to our why questions this side of heaven, but we can choose to trust that God sees clearly. He sees you and knows you *fully.* One day you'll understand a fuller picture. I didn't learn just one lesson from Franje's life; I learned dozens. God is still revealing all the ways He is using Franje's story for good. My prayer for you is that you will begin to keep a lookout for God's presence in the middle of your suffering. I pray you move away from asking why and focus on asking *where.* I pray you will be able to say, "I love You, God! Right now, I can't see how this will work together for good, but I trust it will. Show me how to show up with compassion for others even when I don't feel like it. Make it clear to me where Your silver lining is around this dark cloud hanging over my life. Remind me that I am a part of Your perfect story and that You have never and will never fail me. Amen."

DIG

IN YOUR OWN LIFE

Welcome!

Friend, you already know I want you to get the most out of this book. I want you to put it down feeling lighter and better equipped to face whatever tomorrow brings. So, at the end of each section, you can always expect a **quick recap** of what we've covered so far, along with how it applies to **the big picture** of your life, and then it will be your turn to unpack your own story through some **reflection questions**. There will also be a **challenge** for you to put what you're learning into practice in your everyday life. Finally, there's a suggested **prayer** for you to use as a jumping-off point for talking to God about all this.

Don't rush this process. Carve out some quiet time, free of distractions, to interact with this application section. You can do it all at once or break it into bite size pieces that fit your schedule. This is your turn to be the focus of the story. Be honest with yourself when answering the questions—there's plenty of room to write your responses. Are you ready?

CHECKLIST

My hope for you in Part 1 of the book was for you to:

- Recognize the origin of your confidence.
- Identify unreliable "identity" labels and replace them with truth.
- Embrace God's timing in order to develop a mindset that chooses to trust despite disappointments.
- Be *willing* to take action and wait God's way.
- Understand the power of what a few seconds of compassion can do for people.
- Appreciate the God-wink moments and allow them to fuel you to keep moving.

RECAP

In chapter 1, I shared the end of my reign as Miss Universe, what it took to be crowned, and how I lost self-confidence and rediscovered God-confidence. In the second chapter, we learned that God doesn't operate on our timeline, and while frustrating, waiting helps us make better decisions, toughens our patience posture, and help us see life from a less self-oriented perspective. In chapter 3, through telling the story of my sister, Franje, and her devastating diagnosis, I explored the reality of unmet expectations and seemingly unanswered prayers and the importance of trusting God in the struggle.

THE BIG PICTURE

The world is all about building confidence in the self.

You can do it all!

You already have everything you need!

If you think you can, you will!

Believe in yourself and you can have anything you want!

Statements like these, and many others, are hurled at us through social media, advertisements, and society. Self-confidence is not a bad thing. It's important! We need it to live well, to work hard, to achieve, and to accomplish. But it's not everything. If you hope to live a life of eternal significance, your foundation needs to be anchored in the right place. Understanding the difference between self-confidence and God-confidence is key. Self-confidence, often manufactured from and emphasized by pedigree, looks, vibe, zip code, or social status, is unsustainable in the long run. We all have limitations, after all. Being grounded in God-confidence, however, will level up your living.

God-confidence is about trusting that God is who He says He is according to His Word. It's about believing in His greatness and in His goodness. It's about recognizing and living out the truth that our strength, purpose, and hope come from Him alone. This is what makes us able to climb mountains, find shelter in storms, and face challenges head on. If the promotion doesn't go through, you don't get the number one spot in the class, or a global pandemic throws the world off course, unlike confidence in temporal things, you can trust and rest in God-confidence, which never wanes or wobbles. When life gets tough and sidelines or even rejects your best-laid plans, fix your eyes on God. He created the entire universe. Put your confidence in the One who loves you so much He gave His life for you. The world moves at the words of God. He stitched you together with as much tenderness as my grandma once knit my favorite sweater. You can count on Him!

When you root your confidence in God, you have the right perspective to turn a waiting season into a willing season. As you wait for the job, the degree, the spouse, the family, or the next step, don't just do nothing. Serve. Love. See a need and meet it. Understand that you were created for more than a moment, a marriage, a promotion, a record deal, or to reach a certain number of followers. God wants to use you wherever you are in every season. Step outside of your feelings of frustration or inadequacy to show compassion to others. I know waiting is hard and the days are long, but there are always opportunities to fill that space with prayer, with service, with friendship, and with remembering God's goodness.

Remind yourself that although every prayer may be answered in a way that's different from what you want or expect, you can always experience God's presence. He is with you when the test results cause fear or the breakup grief. Life is full of disappointments, big and small, but what matters most is how we respond to these disappointments. Through overwhelming feelings, tell yourself the promises God gives in Scripture. Instead of backing away from Him, lean into and ask Him to show you His love and purpose when life looks a lot different from what you expected.

Whatever stage of life you're in now, it's never too late to bring your dreams to the Lord, to ask Him to show you His purpose for your life, and to begin to develop a God-confidence!

READ, REFLECT, AND ANSWER

Many of us tend to look at other people or things rather than to God for rescue or relief. Some of us talk our friends to death hoping to find a perfect answer to our problems. Some of us turn to unhealthy habits to numb the pain of disappointment, heartbreak, or confusion. Others try to muster up inner fortitude and grit to get through rough times.

What do you do when your life spins out of control or you get overwhelmed by unanswered prayers? Write down all the coping mechanisms, conscious or unconscious, that you've been relying on:

What are two practical things you can do today to start to shift your focus off of those things/people and actively put your trust in God instead?

1.

2.

The Bible is like a roadmap with the wisdom you need to set your priorities straight, the encouragement you need to keep moving forward, and the discernment you need to make the right decisions, all in one place. So in waiting seasons, there is active power in reading, reflecting on, and memorizing Scripture. Our words may fall short, but the Word of God will never fail (Isaiah 40:8).

Read, reflect on, and memorize Romans 8:38–39:

> For I am convinced that neither death nor life, neither angels nor demons, neither the present nor the future, nor any powers, neither height nor depth, nor anything else in all creation, will

> be able to separate us from the love of God that is in Christ Jesus our Lord.

This verse has given me a lot of comfort over the years. No matter what life throws your way, no matter how many times you've been let down, how busy you've let yourself become, or how unfaithful you feel—this verse reminds us that *not one thing* can separate us from Christ's love. His love is not based on our performance, our talent, our looks, or our intentions. He remains faithful, all the time.

When was the last time you were reminded of the love of God when things got bumpy or went totally off track?

At times waiting on God can seem like wasting, but He never calls us to a season of doing nothing. We can still go to church. Worship. Reach out to others who are going through a painful time. Encourage a friend through phone calls, texts, visits, and prayers. Give our time, our finances, and our talents to impact something or someone for good.

What are three ways you can show God your willingness to work in the waiting?

1.

2.

3.

ACCEPT THE CHALLENGE

One way to stay rooted in God-confidence is by taking the Confidence Swap challenge. For the next seven days, when you are reminded of failures, uncertainty, closed doors, unmet expectations, or disappointments, trade that thought for a God-confidence-charged belief.

TRADE THAT THOUGHT	FOR THIS TRUTH
I am afraid.	God is always with me. He will never leave or forsake me (Deuteronomy 31:6).
I don't know what to do.	The Lord will perfect everything that concerns me in His own timing (Psalm 138:8).
I can't do this.	I can be strong and courageous because God is with me everywhere I go (Joshua 1:9).
I'm not good enough.	You knit me just right inside my mother's body. Everything you do is marvelous! I am perfectly made (Psalm 139:13–14).

PRAYER

(Read this prayer out loud in closing)

> I love You, God! Right now, I can't see how this situation will work together for good, but I trust it will. Show me how to show up with compassion for others even when I don't feel like it. Make it clear to me where Your silver lining is around this dark cloud hanging over my life. Remind me that I am a part of Your perfect story and that You have never and will never fail me. In Jesus' name, amen.

PART TWO

PLANT

I sought the Lord, and he answered me
and rescued me from all my fears.
Those who look to him are radiant with joy;
their faces will never be ashamed.

PSALM 34:4–5 (CSB)

Now that we've successfully dug, it's time to plant! We don't want our labor to go to waste, friend! In my opinion, planting is vital because it symbolizes intentionality and sets us up for growth. What's the point of digging a hole if you're not going to fill it, right? Just as a seed planted in fertile soil has the potential to blossom, I believe when we actively take risks, learn from failure, and take ownership of who God made us to be, we put ourselves in the best position to be used for kingdom impact.

In chapters 4 and 5, we'll challenge the notion that setbacks are the end, and I'll encourage you to create a powerful mindset that anticipates comebacks. You'll also begin to define your own personal brand (convictions, skillset, values, etc.) and resist the pressure of being put in a box. As I discovered pre– and post–Miss Universe, a big part of planting is understanding your personal goals and dreams and the skills you need to develop in order to get you there. In these chapters, my hope is that you're going to:

- Reframe your idea of failure.
- Learn how to distinguish your unique traits and skills from what culture tells you they should be.
- Recognize the people and places God has put you in proximity with.
- Understand the connection between a career and a calling.
- Be inspired to embark on your own mission to discover your vision for your life.

FOUR

EVERY STEP BACK IS A SETUP FOR A STEP-UP

Despite the pain that's been part of our family story, my dad has always been one of the funniest people I know. He is the king of comebacks and one-liners. My friends call him "Papa Bennie" and always look forward to a good laugh when they see him. Funny thing is, he doesn't always get the comeback out because the mere thought of it makes him laugh so hard that he's a goner before he actually gets the joke out. Sometimes I'll just see him cracking up, crying laughing by himself over absolutely nothing, and then I can't help but laugh as well. My abs hurt, my mascara is smudged from the happy tears, and I kinda feel drained from all the laughing. I sometimes wish I could call him in the middle of some banter with my friends to get a good comeback joke. But pausing to ask my dad would probably depreciate the value of a good comeback in the moment, so I've banked a few in my back pocket for future use.

For example, "Your attitude is like a grey sprinkle on a rainbow cupcake."

Or, "That's more disappointing than an unsalted pretzel."

Or one of his classics, "Oh, I'm sorry. Did the middle of my sentence interrupt the beginning of yours?"

Pretty funny, right? Not so funny when you think of the best comeback two hours after the moment is over. Even worse is that lost comeback you never used because you weren't sure if people would find it funny, but when you whisper it to your friend a few minutes later, they cry-laugh.

Missing that perfect opportunity for the witty comeback is kind of like that chance you never took because you weren't sure if it would be a success. Most of the time we'd rather stay stagnant than experience a setback, am I right? But one thing I've learned from my dad and his perfectly timed comebacks is that there is no reward without the risk. If we don't put ourselves out there, knowing it could result in a setback (or a joke that totally flops), then we'll never experience that pure joy of the belly laugh when it's a direct hit.

Everyone loves a good comeback story. I'm not sure why that is, but I think maybe it's because there's nothing sweeter than when someone defeats all odds, breaks all barriers, overcomes all obstacles, and experiences success. But I need to point out that it is *impossible* to make a comeback without the setback; the setback is literally the setup for the success story.

NO RISK, NO REWARD

One of my own favorite comeback stories includes cupcakes, which are really just muffins who believed in miracles and made a major comeback. In my second year in university, I won Miss Varsity Cup.

It was a small competition hosted on campus, and the winner got a few perks like a special parking spot for a year, which is a big deal on any university campus! The title helped me gain a small local following on social media, and back then having five thousand followers felt like you'd "made it."

Not only did winning the competition come with perks, but to me it also came with a sense of responsibility. My heart has been beating for women's safety and empowerment since I was a teenager. Growing up in South Africa, hearing heart-wrenching stories and statistics of violence against women and children broke my heart. Our statistics when it comes to violence against women are sobering. So much so that gender-based violence is viewed as an epidemic in South Africa. According to a 2023 report from the National Library of Medicine, a woman is raped in my home country every *three hours*![1] Even more disturbing is the fact that the rate at which women are killed by domestic partners in South Africa is five times higher than the global average.[2]

And it's not just in South Africa that women face the daily risk of violence. The World Health Organization reported that an estimated one in three women *worldwide* have been subjected to either physical and/or sexual violence in their lifetime.[3] All around the globe, women continue to be seen as objects or commodities for either someone else's fury or pleasure. As a result of these facts, I grew up hypervigilant, always parking close to my classes (even if it meant I would get a parking ticket). I never walked alone and instead stayed with a group of girlfriends or stuck with a guy friend. And I always left campus before sunset. I knew many girls who felt the same way and feared that they would become one of the statistics we all read about.

I didn't want to live with the constant anxiety of not knowing how to properly look out for myself; I wanted to know how to act wisely in an unwanted situation. So I completed several self-defense workshops as well as multiple secure driving courses to be able to protect myself from a car-jacking or other safety concern on the road.

I've always been passionate about women empowering other women, so it was only natural that I wanted to use the opportunity as Miss Varsity Cup to mentor and empower the girls on my campus. My goal was to provide them (with the help of field experts) with the same tangible knowledge on how to physically protect themselves, emotionally protect themselves, and create a powerful mindset. My hope was that each student would leave feeling better equipped to face everyday challenges—dark parking lots, nerve-racking tests, conflicts in relationships, and even financial woes. Coming up with a game plan and finding a resolution to an issue instead of feeling paralyzed by fear seemed like a noble endeavor. So I decided to host a women's empowerment workshop.

I had no idea what I was supposed to be doing to make it a successful event. The vision I had and my ability to execute it as a nineteen-year-old were miles apart. For example, I used a Wonder Woman logo in a very low-quality, budget-friendly design app to design pamphlets and some graphics for social media to hype up the event. I visited two or three sororities to invite girls to my empowerment event and convinced our university to lend me their 3,500-seat auditorium for half a day. I somehow even got them to let me use their foyer space to host a special VIP teatime after the conference. I'm still not sure who I thought these Very Important People were going to be. Ha! Demi had big dreams! I asked a local grocery store to donate paper products for the tea, as well as, you guessed it, cupcakes! I had no way of knowing how many people would actually attend our pop-up teatime and figured thirty cupcakes would be enough.

Imagine my surprise when I arrived at the grocery store the day before the event to pick up the cupcakes, and the store owner asked me if I'd brought a pickup truck to transport the goods. I couldn't tell if he was joking or making fun of my amateur event-hosting skills. "Um, I'm sure everything will fit in my car," I replied. The store owner just stared at me like I had no idea what I was talking about. Then he turned around and disappeared into a doorway without saying a word. As I stood between a few loaves of bread and some cakes, I wasn't sure what to do next. My instinct was to wait. A few minutes later, the owner came walking through the doors pulling a large baking trolley with about ten large shelves. Packed. With. Cupcakes! I quickly realized we'd had a communication problem. While I'd asked for thirty cupcakes, he had prepared thirty *dozen*, or 360 cupcakes. Sadly, on the day of my event, ten times more cupcakes than people showed up. Half the people who attended were my friends and family. Looking back, it's laughable that I thought my few pamphlets and Instagram posts and a paltry speaker lineup would draw enough people to fill 3,500 seats. Live events are not for the faint of heart, y'all! On another funny note, let's just say we were eating frozen leftover cupcakes for a very long time!

While you might think the whole cupcake debacle would have dampened my desire to create this self-defense workshop, it did not. Three years later I relaunched and rebranded my women's empowerment event, this time using my Miss South Africa title. With more clarity around what it would entail, better planning, a new title, and a team to help me, it's safe to say more *people* than cupcakes showed up the second time around. I named this women's empowerment workshop "Unbreakable." What had started as a project at university by a girl who didn't want to become another statistic evolved into a confidence-building conference, empowering women across the world in all aspects of life: mentally, physically, and emotionally. We brought in world-renowned, boss-lady field experts to help equip our audience with confidence through knowledge and education.

Today, Unbreakable is going stronger than ever. At the first post-pandemic Unbreakable workshop hosted in the US, we had more than five hundred women attend. That is forty dozen more women than attended my amateur original workshop back in 2015! Now the thirty dozen cupcakes would've been a shortage!

Back then it would've been so much easier to gorge on cupcakes and give up on the event that only my friends, family, and a few bored girls attended. But where's the fun in that? No challenge; no change. No risk; no reward. When we don't give up, our best next choice is to put on our big girl panties, woman up, and find a way to make things work.

When trying something new, it's important to understand that succeeding the first time is very rare. According to researchers, only 9 percent of Americans who make New Year's resolutions achieve them.[4] The U.S. Small Business Administration reports that roughly 20 percent of startups fail in their first year, 50 percent fail within five years, and two-thirds fail within ten years.[5] Did you know that James Dyson created 5,126 failed prototypes before creating his successful vacuum cleaner?[6] Thomas Edison failed ten thousand times before creating a successful lightbulb.[7] In Thomas Edison's often-quoted words, "I have not failed. I've just found ten thousand ways that won't work," we realize that we are not alone in our failures.[8] These statistics confirm that failure is actually a part of the process when creating anything of value. I mean, if Thomas Edison gave up, I'd be sitting here writing to you with pen and paper by candlelight! This should remind and empower us to pick ourselves back up and try again. This kind of tenacity is what makes a comeback story so admirable.

Listen, life is always going to throw a wrench in our plans. There will always be obstacles, failures, and setbacks to overcome. When it comes to other people's success, we don't see the ten thousand hours of failure that came beforehand. But when it comes to our own obstacles, our brains can latch onto the idea that our challenges are one of a kind. *No one else is going through what I am, and no one else understands what it's like.* This is a kind of self-protection. I get it. But when we believe that our battles are isolated, we tend to stay stuck, justifying the loss to ourselves. While there are definitely "one in a million" situations out there, most of the battles we face, others have faced before us. We can take strength and comfort from that fact. Plenty of people have walked in similar shoes as you and still found a way to turn their pain into power and their setbacks into opportunities. These are the comeback stories where we see how the challenge initiated the change; how the risk taken led to reward.

KEEP COMING BACK

> The tragedy of life does not lie in not reaching your goals;
> The tragedy of life lies in not having goals to reach for.[9]

This quote is from a poem by Benjamin Mays, which also happens to be the same poem Natalie du Toit would carry with her for an inspirational boost before swim meets (laminated, of course, so it didn't get wet). I don't know how many of you are familiar with Natalie's story, but it's one of the most inspirational comeback stories I heard growing up in South Africa. What could have been a dream-crushing setback became a powerful stepping stone to the life of her dreams, giving hope and courage to people with disabilities all over the world.

At age fourteen, Natalie represented South Africa at the 1998

Commonwealth Games, swimming in the 400m Individual Medley and 200m Butterfly races. Natalie was a swimming prodigy with her heart set on competing at the Olympics. But just three years later, Natalie lost her lower left leg in a tragic scooter accident. What could have been the most devastating setback to end all her dreams of becoming an Olympic swimmer became a set*up* not only for accomplishing her dreams, but also finding a deeper purpose.

Despite the pain, Natalie persevered through her recovery process with a positive attitude and the same end goal in mind: to become an Olympian. She said, "I put it down to faith—things happen for a reason. And, as it happens, this has opened other doors for me."[10] This is such a great reminder that God has a purpose in the pain, and He can redeem every setback we encounter if we lean in and let Him.

Only three months after her amputation (and before she started walking again), Natalie was back in the pool. Within one year she went on to win two of the multi-disability races in world record time at the 2002 Commonwealth Games. Natalie's identity wasn't rooted in her life-altering setback. Instead, she saw it as a challenge to overcome rather than something that defined her. At the age of twenty-one, only three years after the accident, Natalie accomplished her dream of becoming an Olympic swimmer, competing in the 2004 Paralympic Games in Athens. But it doesn't stop there. Natalie didn't let the loss of her leg dictate her future or define who she was. She qualified to participate in the 2008 Beijing Olympics against able-bodied athletes![11] Wow! Talk about a comeback. Fast-forward to today: she is a sought-after motivational speaker who shares lessons about facing adversity and finding the silver linings in bad situations by refusing to let setbacks become one's defining characteristic.

I don't know Natalie on a deep, personal level, but I imagine she had a lot of bad days, a lot of fear and doubt when getting back into the water. I'm sure that year of recovery and adjusting to a new lifestyle was anything but easy. She may have wanted to give up along the way. But through her faith, she was determined to not let her setback be the final word in her life.

The comeback isn't a once-off thing. It's the active choice of "coming back" over and over again that displays your character and faith. Some of you might be in a season of coming back. You've faced obstacles and setbacks, and received no after no after no. Despite the pushback, are you leaning into your faith and coming back anyway?

It feels like there are so many great comeback examples in sports I could offer, but I find myself thinking of my dad, who left his comfortable corporate job to spend more time at home to help care for Franje. To replace his income, my dad made a plan and converted a portion of our home, including our garages, into guest rooms. They made our family comeback possible, even though it meant sharing our living room with strangers for two years. He now owns and runs a successful fifteen-bedroom bed-and-breakfast property.

I think of my mom, who didn't graduate high school but learned everything she could about the industry she got her first job in and then founded her own Rand company that employed dozens of other people, regardless of whether they had a high school diploma, never mind a college degree. I think of our friends, who could not conceive for eight years, and now have a beautiful family of four. I think of our pastor, who started a small church gathering out of obedience despite not having funding or a building and now runs a megachurch. I think of one of my best friends' moms who followed an extremely healthy lifestyle but got cancer regardless, beat the cancer, and now helps guide other patients through their cancer journeys.

If you feel like you are facing an impossible circumstance in your life or a barrier that feels too high to overcome, be encouraged by the stories of people just like you who are figuring it out not with the best resources or qualifications, but with the determination to get back up again.

WHAT BLOCKS OUR BELIEF IN COMEBACKS?

I think most of us hear stories like Natalie's and still feel like our comeback is as out of reach as that European vacation we've been dreaming about. It got me thinking, *Why is it so hard to believe in our own comeback?* While there might be a million reasons, five stand out to me based on my own experience, the many stories I've heard, and the research I've done.

1. We indulge in self-pity.

Yes. I said it. One of the major reasons we focus on the setbacks instead of believing in the possibility of a comeback is because we can get bogged down in pity about the results at the "halftime" of what we set out to do. I felt lost and stranded between countries and opportunities after my year as Miss Universe. Trust me when I tell you I could have thrown an epic pity party, cupcakes and all! I know exactly how it feels to get so upset that the "first half" didn't go my way or that things didn't go as planned. I understand the temptation to give up on figuring out a way to move forward and give in to stewing over all the reasons that things went wrong. It might make us feel better in the short term, but it's not a long-term solution to focus on the downside of a crummy first half. Instead, focus on seeing the upside of the second half.

I can channel my inner toddler like the best of them, but the truth is that sulking in self-pity leads to blaming others, isolation, negative self-talk, victim mentality, and refusing help when we need it most. Overcoming this tendency to wallow is essential to believing in successful comebacks!

2. It's easier to give up.

I know we can all relate to this one. The Britannica Dictionary tells us that "to *give up* means to stop trying to do something because you are not having success doing it."[12] Literally, it is easier to just stop doing something than to keep going once you've fallen behind. When our brains get tired, it's harder to keep making choices that require willpower. Add to that the fact that when you're low on confidence, your brain kicks into gear trying to protect you from discouragement and then tells you to quit to protect your feelings. Yup, our own brains go into fight-or-flight mode against us and choose flight to protect us from our own negative emotions.

There's a good amount of science that explains this reaction. In short, when things get tough, our bodies produce a stress hormone called cortisol, which is supposed to help mobilize our energy reserves and temporarily suppress the immune system during times of stress. However, excessive cortisol production brought on by that rough first half—whether that looks like ongoing financial worries, relationship problems, work-related stress, poor sleep, a business plan that is falling apart, or that teenager who is pushing our last buttons—can result in a range of negative health effects, making us feel anxious and frustrated.[13] This can make any task seem even harder, pushing us to quit to get some relief.

Think about running that five-mile race; you realize that you are far behind. You're tired, not as fit as you wanted to be, and you see no way that you could possibly catch up to win a medal. It's easier to back out and eat a burger than to finish the race you started. Personally,

I am so competitive that it works to my disadvantage sometimes. If I think I can't win, I've been known to opt out of participating. But even if we don't break the record, write a dozen books, or become the president, we still get to find joy and learn about ourselves in the process of participating. Sometimes we even surprise ourselves with talents we never knew we had or discover that we enjoy things we never thought we would. And the truth is, finishing when all the odds have been stacked against us is the deepest kind of satisfaction.

3. Our brain chemicals hold us back.

Humans are not created to naturally enjoy losing or failing, and neither are our brains. Have you ever started a day feeling *excited* about the possibility of being disappointed? Yeah, me neither. If we face problems or think we're not getting anywhere, our brains react strongly, making us more likely to give up to avoid feeling like we've failed. You have a built-in calculator in your brain that figures out if the benefits of finishing a task are worth the effort. If your brain thinks the cost of finishing is too high, it might simply advise you to stop.[14]

But there's another chemical at work in your decision-making. Even if you've never heard the word *dopamine*, you've definitely *felt* its effects. Dopamine is a feel-good chemical released in your brain that allows you to experience pleasure. It's a way for your body to tell you, "Yay, I love this!" Whether having a good time with friends, eating great food, or exercising, it's an amazing chemical God created for you and me to experience joy and happiness. However, dopamine can be suppressed. In a recent University of Washington study, researchers looked at the neurons in mice seeking a sugary treat by poking their snout into a port. At first, it was easy, but then it became increasingly harder as they had to poke more times to get the treat. Eventually, the mice stopped trying.

Researchers discovered that inside the mice's brain, a group of cells known as nociception neurons got very active before a mouse's breakpoint. These cells essentially release a molecule that suppresses the "feel good" chemical, dopamine. When things got tough, and the mice felt like giving up, there were neurons that worked *against* their motivation to keep going. Imagine you're trying to run but somebody is holding on to the back of your shirt, pulling against you and prohibiting your effort to run forward. That's what's happening here. Our motivation to persist in difficult situations is held back by a chemical reaction that stops the "feel good" hormone (dopamine) from releasing. The neurons found in mice and humans share many similarities, therefore researchers are beginning to believe that this finding could apply to humans.[15]

4. We fear *more* failure or *future* failure.

This phenomena can also play a pivotal role in this reluctance to believe in comebacks. Moses, a pretty significant figure in the Old Testament, initially hesitated and expressed fear when God called him to lead the Israelites out of slavery in Egypt. If you can remember from Sunday school, Moses was the guy who killed an Egyptian man in an attempt to deliver his own people from the hand of Pharaoh. But instead of rallying the enslaved Israelites at that time, they rebuked him, saying, "Who made you ruler and judge over us? Are you thinking of killing me as you killed the Egyptian?" (Exodus 2:14). Tough day. Not only did Moses feel rejected, but he also ran away to a distant land in hopes of never stepping foot in Egypt again.

Fast-forward forty years when Moses was eighty. God appeared to him through the burning bush and tasked him with a monumental mission: *return* to Egypt. Deeply concerned about his ability to succeed, Moses responded to God's call by saying, "Who am I that I should go to Pharaoh and bring the Israelites out of Egypt?"

(Exodus 3:11). Here in such a divine moment, Moses was worried about his own inadequacy. He was essentially telling God, "I've already tried to rescue your people and I failed. Why should I go back? I'll just make it worse!" But that's not all. Later in the conversation Moses raised concerns about not being persuasive enough or capable enough (Exodus 4:10). Isn't this so interesting and typical? When we've experienced failure, not only do we resist trying again, but we also begin to doubt our own skillset and abilities. In a moment that would eventually change Israel's history forever, Moses didn't want to believe in a comeback! He was too concerned with causing more collateral damage.

5. We lack belief.

Struggling to believe in a comeback is actually rooted in belief itself. Stay with me here; twentieth-century innovator and the father of the automobile, Henry Ford, is commonly quoted as saying, "Whether you believe you can or whether you believe you cannot, you're right."[16] In essence, this statement by Ford emphasizes the profound impact your beliefs have on your results. If you believe you can achieve something, you're more likely to succeed; conversely, if you believe you can't, you're more likely to fail. In many ways, your expectations and mindset greatly influence your outcomes.

For believers, I think we can take that one step further. When we lack belief, we inadvertently make God *small*. When we believe we can't make a comeback, we're saying God isn't capable of a comeback either. I don't want to be someone who believes in a *small* God. As my pastor says, "If the tomb is empty, *anything* is possible."[17]

In Acts 12, we find one of Jesus' three closest disciples, Peter, sitting in a prison cell, guarded under heavy security. While Peter waited in prison—potentially facing death the next morning—the Christians in Jerusalem prayed "fervently to God for him" (v. 5 CSB).

Keep that in mind. The church was *praying* for him. That night, God showed up in a miraculous way to help Peter escape his cell. Once free, Peter ran to meet up with his friends who had been praying. Look what happened next:

> When [Peter] knocked at the door of the gate, a servant-girl named Rhoda came to answer. When she recognized Peter's voice, because of her joy she did not open the gate, but ran in and announced that Peter was standing in front of the gate. They said to her, "You are out of your mind!" But she kept insisting that it was so. They kept saying, "It is his angel." But Peter continued knocking; and when they had opened the door, they saw him and were amazed. (Acts 12:13–16 NASB1995)

Two things I love about this passage. One, Rhoda is my girl! When she heard Peter's voice, she got so excited she forgot to open the door! Hearing her giddiness and footsteps scurrying away, Peter probably sarcastically thought, *Sweet, I'll just wait here*. The second thing I love is Rhoda's faith. When she shared the news that their friend was *not behind bars*, nobody believed her. They said, "You're out of your mind." The Greek here even suggests they thought she was mad, a crazy person as if demon possessed.[18] But Rhoda was right! Peter was there!

What's crazy is that these Christians were praying for something—most likely for Peter's release and protection—but none of them besides Rhoda actually believed God had answered when Peter showed up on their doorstep. Rhoda wasn't out of her mind; she just believed in a *big* God because she had seen His kind of comeback with her own eyes. Whatever roadblock you're facing and whatever restricts the possibility of your comeback, I hope you take courage from the people who've stood in your shoes. I hope you follow in their footsteps, believing that there are ways for you to overcome what you're facing.

THE POWER OF A POWERFUL MINDSET

Now that we've walked through some of the reasons it's so hard for us to believe in our own comeback, it's time to start equipping ourselves with the tools to overcome the doubt, fear, and even those pesky brain chemicals. I'm going to walk you through three practical steps to build a powerful mindset, and it starts with the *mind.*

1. Reframe your identity.

Dr. Caroline Leaf, a South African communication pathologist and neuroscientist, pioneered the study of deliberate mental activities and their impact on brain change.[19] Our beliefs make up our *identity* and influence our mindset (for better or worse), often leading to self-doubt rooted in insecurities stemming from fears of failure, success, and judgment. Healing and rewriting these memories offer a path to crafting a more empowering narrative and overcoming self-doubt.[20]

Looking back I realized that initially being fearful to host another Unbreakable workshop stemmed from the knock to my ego after the first one was a bit of an embarrassment when basically nobody showed up. I get to look at that event and be proud of my attempt as a nineteen-year-old and see it as an opportunity to grow, learn, and be better next time. Reframing our identity does not mean we rewrite the truth. Reframing our identity is a healing journey that reprocesses the past to make sense of the present moment to embrace a healthy personal identity.

The healing journey doesn't happen overnight. It takes time.

When we do the work to help reframe our setbacks and the hard things in our past, we start to see ourselves the way God sees us. From there, we can start to visualize our comeback on the path ahead, which is a victory in and of itself.

2. Let go so you can move forward.

Can you release what is holding you back or weighing you down? Can you let that burden go? If you can, you're creating emotional, mental, and spiritual space to reevaluate what is best to do moving forward. It's like that one cluttered closet in your house (okay, fine, maybe two) that's full of things you've been holding on to *just in case* you might need them. Let's be honest, you're never going to wear that bridesmaid's dress again. You have more woven baskets than your favorite home goods store. You really don't need those books you read a decade ago. And you certainly don't want that nasty-smelling candle in your home.

By getting rid of the dress and donating a bunch of those old baskets, bins, and books that have been piling up for years, you're creating room for something new. Maybe you transform that cupboard into an art closet, or how about a makeup closet with mirrors and organizational bins (putting that on my list!). What's important here is that letting go of the clutter makes room for reevaluation. In other words, letting go is not the same as giving up. Letting go is what makes room to let something else in.

3. Trust that God's got this.

Our setbacks in life may catch us by surprise, but they never surprise God. God knows everything about you! Your faults, failures, feelings, frustrations, fears, friends, and future. He knows what your yesterday looked like and what your tomorrow holds. He knows the pain you've experienced, the insecurities you wrestle with, the places you love to visit, the habits you hope to drop, the thoughts you have at night, the number of times you hit snooze in the morning, and the songs you sing in the shower. The psalmist put it like this: "Before there is a word on my tongue, Behold, O LORD, You know it all" (Psalm 139:4 NASB1995). God possesses complete knowledge of your imperfections, mistakes, emotions, and struggles, as well as what awaits you in the days to come. The Bible says that before you were born, God knew all of your future: "Your eyes saw my unformed body; all the days ordained for me were written in your book before one of them came to be" (Psalm 139:16). How beautiful. He knows it all; therefore, *nothing* can catch God by surprise!

As many times as we get surprised by life's setbacks or unexpected hardships that seemingly pop up out of nowhere—a global pandemic, a market crash, divorce papers, a bad diagnosis, a backhanded comment from a friend, a flight delay, or a flat tire—when it comes to our circumstances, they don't surprise Him. God's omniscience and omnipotence transcend the bounds of time and circumstance. And I'm not just talking about the things that come our way unexpectedly that God has foreknowledge of. I find a lot of peace knowing that even though God knows the mistakes I'll make down the road, it doesn't affect His love or His plan for me.

Throughout the gospels, one of Jesus' closest friends and followers, Peter, is often remembered as a reckless man with a big mouth. From doubting Jesus' power while walking on the Sea of Galilee (Matthew 14:22–33) to being compared to Satan for being a hindrance to God's plan (16:21–23) and then denying his relationship with Jesus three times (26:33–35), Peter's humanity is one I can relate to. I resonate with some of Peter's prideful, fearful, and irrational behavior. But what I love about Peter's life is that despite all his setbacks, God wasn't caught off guard and still decided to use Peter for His glory!

We get a glimpse into this in the book of John when, after a very intimate breakfast on the beach, the resurrected Christ reassured and restored Peter's calling as a leader of the future church (John 21). All of Peter's shortcomings were no surprise to God. Rather, He eventually used Peter's big mouth to preach the first Christian sermon in Jerusalem on the day of Pentecost, and around three thousand people were saved that day (Acts 2:41).

God will equip you for where He has called you. In the meantime, embrace your middle zone by stepping up in obedience and acting on what you're called to do. You can do hard things not because of your abilities but because you serve a limitless God who multiplies the little we have to offer Him to feed thousands.

A HALFTIME SPEECH TO REMEMBER

You guys know I'm South African; therefore, American football wasn't a part of my childhood. It wasn't even on my radar. I'm a *rugby* girl. But one of my favorite halftime speeches comes from a football game (yes, I'm biased). The Florida Gators were tied 7–7 at halftime of the 2009 BCS National Championship against the number-one-rated Oklahoma Sooners. They needed a comeback to win. Picture my husband, Tim Tebow, busting through the locker room huddle and yelling,

> We've got thirty minutes for the rest of our lives. Thirty minutes for the rest of our lives. That's our bad in the first half. It ain't happening. We get the ball, I promise you one thing. We're going to hit somebody, and we're taking it down the field for a touchdown. I guarantee you that . . . .We got thirty minutes for the rest of our lives. Let's go!

They had trained all season for that game. They believed they were the better team, but their performance during the first half was not showing it. Tim's challenge to his team before they stepped back out onto the field was essentially this: "For thirty more minutes, let's put it all on the line to get the win!"

They ended up winning the National Championship, and the Gators 2009 team went down in football history as one of the greatest college football teams of our time. (Once again, very biased!) Regardless of who your favorite teams are, I think we can all agree that Tim had a great point. The Gators did not allow their first-half setback to determine their destiny. They persevered, showed up stronger, beat the odds, and won that National Championship trophy.

I was so inspired by Tim's speech that day and thought we needed our own halftime speech to get us through our own setbacks and on to victory. So repeat after me:

> My setbacks, my failures, or the times I've fallen short
> do not define my destiny.
> They will not get the final say.
> God created me for so much more. I believe it because
> I've seen it.
> God placed a dream in my heart, and I will not give
> up until I experience victory.
> Victory God's way.
> My setbacks are just setups for my ultimate comeback.
> And to those of you watching, buckle up, take a seat,
> and take notes.
> I was made for such a time as this.

Can I get an amen! Sometimes life may seem like a steep uphill climb, on a bicycle, in the rain, with a flat tire. But as we live and grow, we learn that the obstacles and challenges we face can each be an opportunity in disguise. The people who choose to rise up in the face of adversity despite the challenge or setback don't have a superhuman ability or some special advantage; they just believe in the possibility of a comeback.

Your setbacks don't define you; how you respond to those setbacks does. It's not going to be easy. You may have to stumble and fall; you may get a little bruised along the way. But what sets you apart will be your resilience, your unwavering belief that no matter how tough things get, with Jesus, you have the power to overcome and rise again. So next time you face adversity, your plans fail, or you have to start again, remember these important words: "This setback is just a setup for my comeback."

FIVE

YOU ARE YOUR OWN CEO

I'd like to introduce you to a statement that completely changed the way I carry myself. Whether you're an intern, director, baker, artist, or social media influencer, there is one central and empowering key that applies to whatever you do, wherever you are:

You are your own CEO.

Before I start breaking this statement down, I want to clarify something important. Being your own CEO does not mean that you are all-powerful, all-capable, have full autonomy over your life, or that anything you put your mind to is possible. Being your own CEO simply means taking ownership of who God created you to be and not cracking under the pressure from the world to be or act a certain way. Instead, you walk boldly in the identity you have in your Maker and trust that with Him all things are possible.

In chapter 2 we essentially talked about getting our hearts in the right place. Chapter 4 focused on getting our minds in the right place, and in this chapter we are going to learn to get our butts in the right place. That's right, friend. Even though God has a perfect plan for our lives, chances of that perfect plan coming to fruition are slim if all we're doing is sitting on the couch watching Netflix. Listen, I love a good binge as much as the next girl, but the reality is that to live in your purpose, you still have to show up with a willing heart, an intent mindset, and an eager spirit to run to wherever He's called you.

I first discovered this concept of being my own CEO when I was asked to speak to a group of ladies at a business workshop. The theme of the event was something like "how to be successful." This was a daunting speaking topic that I felt extremely unequipped to speak on at the age of twenty-two. There were actual business mentors and successful business owners in the audience. I wish they had asked me to give a talk on "how to dress for success" or "how to ace your interview." To add more pressure, I was asked to encourage the ladies and leave them feeling inspired and motivated to work toward reaching their career goals, which were wide and varied in this diverse group of women. Most of the attendees had lived challenging lives. Some were single mothers, some had criminal records, some had a lot of work experience, and others had none.

Before my turn to speak, I joined some of the attendees for lunch. At first I was hesitant; I was tempted to sit backstage and work on my talk a little longer. But I'm so glad I didn't hide away. Lunch was transformational. By the end of it, I'd thrown out my whole speech because I learned something way more valuable by spending time with those sweet ladies. I got to know them on a personal level and learned more about their dreams. I met a secretary, a schoolteacher, first-time business owners, women who were working their way up the corporate ladder, and women who were completing their GED or applying to colleges for the first time. Every attendee was unique and possessed a unique set of skills, yet everyone had one common ability. Light-bulb moment! It dawned on me that no matter your position in a company or in society, we all have the ability to be our own CEO.

According to the Cambridge Dictionary, *CEO* is an "abbreviation for chief executive officer: the person with the most important position in a company."[1] Basically, it's the person in charge of making sure that there is a plan, that people are executing the plan, and that everything is going according to plan.

Of course, not all of us will be an actual CEO in charge of a company, but we can be in charge of setting our own strategic direction for our lives, just like each of the women at that luncheon were doing. You can take charge of the ins and outs of running the company that collectively makes up *you*. That means you are in charge of overseeing the marketing department, the finance department, and the operations it takes to efficiently run your world. You are in charge of the way you carry yourself and the first impressions you make. You can decide whether to show up on time, do the research, and prep your questions. You can decide to create routines for yourself that help you be more efficient with your time. You can choose to cancel those unused subscriptions or make coffee at home so you can put more into your daughter's college fund. No matter what you do for a living, you oversee your brand identity.

With the onset of social media influencers, the phrases "defining your personal brand" or "creating your brand identity" have become pretty buzzworthy topics. But creating your personal brand isn't just for influencers; it's a big part of becoming your own CEO and taking control of your next step. Creating your own "brand identity" is my fun way of saying, "Here are the parameters you should use to help determine your next steps." Know your passions, principles, desired reputation, strengths, endearments, nonnegotiables, ideal legacy, how you are perceived, and what sets you apart to discover your brand identity.

Basically, I'm proposing that we follow the example of new companies by discovering our brand identity first, then building out our product lines (expanding on our unique set of skills and talents), marketing strategies (our way of communicating what we have to offer), and resources (things that will make us better, like an online workshop, a Bible study leader, a mentor) around that. Take the time to understand what your strengths are and what services you want to offer. You can't rightly represent something if you haven't taken the time to understand the assignment. Plant your stake in the ground for who you think God is calling you to be as you serve alongside Him.

THE BIRTH OF A CEO THROUGH TOILET PAPER AND CUPCAKES

I didn't realize it then, but I think the first time that the idea of taking charge of my personal brand came about was when I was in boarding school. When you think of "boarding school," you probably envision an old building, screechy steel beds with bad mattresses, girls waiting in line for a shower stall while yelling at each other to hurry up! Scary hallways, strict rules, uniforms, and girl drama. The ultimate organized chaos. I wish I could tell you differently, but that was exactly my boarding school experience.

I went to boarding school for two main reasons. My hometown did not have a high school, and the nearest one was an hour away. No way any reasonable parent would drive four hours a day for their kid's school. Homeschooling wasn't an option since I preferred being with a group of kids and was active in sports. You would check into boarding school on Sunday nights or Monday mornings, depending on how far away you lived. Some girls would stay for a couple of weeks before going home if they lived far away.

The dorm girls were given one day a week (Wednesday afternoons) to go into town to pick up necessities like toiletries or forbidden foods like McDonald's. We had to make sure we packed appropriately for the week ahead before arriving at check-in, including snacks, toiletries, and toilet paper. Yup, we were responsible for bringing our own toilet paper. Kind of a disaster if you forgot that or ran out. And believe me, many girls forgot to pack it!

This is where the entrepreneur in me was born. I've heard it said that successful entrepreneurs are just people who identify a problem everyone is facing and create a solution. But first came the snacks. By midweek, many girls would run out of their snacks, including me. A bunch of teenagers with sugar cravings set me up for the perfect first-ever dormitory-run bakery. Okay, I'm exaggerating. But I did start selling cupcakes from underneath my dorm bed. Genius! I saw a problem and created a profitable solution. You're probably thinking, "What's with this girl and cupcakes?!" I sold the other girls cupcakes, which I baked on Sundays at home, out of a big cardboard box wrapped with cling paper. It was totally dodgy looking, especially after traveling from my hometown and enduring a day or two of cling wrap that got stuck on the icing. The cupcakes were just the start though.

Once my cupcake business took off, thanks to word of mouth and great hallway reviews, I established a reputable brand for myself. I was able to take a risk and launch a second product category. You guessed it—toilet paper. Cupcakes and toilet paper. If you needed either, I was your girl! But it would cost you. Listen, it wasn't an easy business! Cupcakes and TP don't really go together, so advertising was a challenge. Some might say my business had a major brand identity crisis, but I think it was pretty genius.

I didn't make a lot of money from my side hustle, but I learned how important it is to take advantage of the opportunities right in front of you. I learned how hard it is to earn people's trust, build a good reputation, take calculated risks, and how to value those loyal to you. The biggest lesson was what I learned about myself through the process. I learned that I liked running a business and wanted to learn more about it. I enjoyed working with people but didn't love the baking part. I loved the challenge of selling all my cupcakes before Wednesday every week, so I didn't lose out on sales from everyone being able to replenish their own snacks in town. I learned to stick to my gut even when others didn't understand my vision. I could've spent a lot of time, effort, and energy coming up with a plan to sell a wider variety of baked goods, but I wasn't in the business of selling the cutest cupcakes or the softest toilet paper. I was in the business of fulfilling a need that could not be met elsewhere. I think the key to my success (for my small boarding-school side hustle) was believing in myself, not listening to the opinions of other people, and not letting other people pressure me into pursuing other paths that weren't a part of my bigger vision, like selling potato chips, soda, or worse . . . hair ties.

Even though I didn't listen to the "haters" at boarding school with their opinions around my odd product choices, that doesn't mean I haven't fallen prey to those pressures or expectations from other people throughout my life. I've had my moments when I saw a comment or heard a statement that made me completely doubt myself. I've even let comments from complete strangers affect me, and it makes me mad at myself even remembering it!

One of those moments happened when accompanying Tim to a speaking engagement shortly after getting married. Backstage, one of the sweet ladies in the meet-and-greet line asked me, "Now what? Do you have any hobbies? How are you going to keep yourself busy on the road seeing that you married such a busy man?" She had no idea what my background was or who I was at all. I want to believe that she had no ill intent and that she grew up in a generation where it was believed that women should be seen and not heard, dedicating their lives to caring for their husbands. But without even realizing it, she had slapped a big, fat sticky label on my forehead that read, "Tim Tebow's Wife." Her words made me question myself and my role as a new wife. It made me wonder if pursuing my own career was the right thing to do. Thoughts rushed through my mind: *Wait, am I supposed to drop everything and become a stay-at-home wife so that I can only support my husband? Will I be a failure as a wife if I don't? Should I just be Tim Tebow's Wife for the rest of my life?*

One person's question caused me to briefly spiral into self-doubt. This was a big fat trap set up by the Enemy, who feeds us lies to make us doubt who we are. It's easy to let go of things we cannot touch; therefore, it's also easy to give up on our God-given identity when we haven't taken the time to engrain the only label that matters, our God-given label, onto our hearts. It's usually in those vulnerable moments when our self-confidence is shaken the most. I was new at the whole "being a wife" thing and needed to remind myself who Tim married. Don't get me wrong. Having found my life partner and getting to cheer him on every day are two of my life's greatest blessings. At the same time, marriage isn't the only purpose in my life. I knew that shifting my confidence in my crown to putting my meaning in my marriage wasn't going to give me an everlasting identity.

KINGDOM OVER BRAND

Much like my newlywed identity-crisis debacle, when we're not confident in our identity and our self-confidence is shaken, it's so much easier to believe and buy into the pressure others put on us. Navigating our identity in light of a new season takes time. Whether it's a new career or a new title, we're not always sure who we are in light of this change, leaving us vulnerable to those external pressures or expectations.

For me, it was the year following my Miss Universe reign. During that waiting season, I signed with a large international modeling agency in New York City. Most former Miss Universes become models, actors, or TV personalities, so I assumed I was right on track. For any serious model, signing with a big agency means you've essentially "made it." I was the first Miss Universe to ever sign a modeling contract with this specific agency. I was feeling those "you're crushing it, girl!" vibes. I had been placed on a pedestal as Miss Universe and believed I was supposed to stay on that pedestal after my reign. I was on the "right" path as far as the world goes, but somehow that path didn't feel *right*.

In order to make it in this very competitive industry, I attended multiple castings for modeling and TV commercial shoots. I only needed *one* big modeling campaign to build my portfolio and essentially "put me on the map." I was told that because of my short height and "sporty" build, lingerie or swimsuit modeling would be the best option for me. I didn't fit in the high-fashion or runway model box. Hesitantly, I attended lingerie and bathing suit castings, wondering, *Is this what I really want?* But I then convinced myself that *it's my only way forward to achieve success.*

Success. I thought I had already achieved that by winning Miss Universe. I thought I had reached the pinnacle of beauty, only to discover another ladder I was told to climb. It was discouraging to realize the finish line kept moving. On the one hand, I had interviews with the number one brand in that market. Working with that company would have put me on track to becoming an international supermodel. I had the opportunity to be "someone" after being Miss Universe. It was a lucrative opportunity. A clear path up the rungs of success. So I told myself, *It's not a big deal, right? It's just a bikini shoot. I wear a bikini on the beach all the time. Do I even have a choice?* My options seemed limited. The industry expected me to keep climbing or get out.

It didn't feel the way I thought it would or should. I didn't feel fulfilled, and I longed for something different. My name, image, and likeness would be used to make brands money, and my identity would be rooted in what they thought my value was: my body, my external appearance, my ability to sell an image of their idea of a woman. Deep in my soul, I knew this kind of "success" couldn't give me the lasting fulfillment I deeply longed for. I didn't realize it at the time, but that "different" I was searching for was *my eternal identity.*

Discovering the desire for a deeper purpose, knowing that my life had more meaning than just making money for a brand, was a key catalyst to understanding this "you are your own CEO" concept. I realized that you can't take charge of your life or define your brand identity if you don't understand who you were created to be and the plan your Creator has for you.

I attended an event in Minnesota that would clarify this difference for me. I arrived at the church early, and the event hosts were so kind to let me use one of the pastor's vacant offices as a green room to go over my notes and fix my glued-on eyelash that never wanted to stick. I couldn't help but notice the gigantic whiteboard that covered the office wall. In the corner of the whiteboard only three words were written: "Kingdom over Brand." These three simple words couldn't have been more awakening. I thought, *Yes, that's right. It should be that way. You go, pastor. Whoever wrote that, amen! Kingdom over Brand.*

I know how easy it is to get caught up in building the business, building the brand, and forgetting about the kingdom impact. I grew up thinking that you can't mix business and purpose. That it was too complicated. That business is business. Purpose is philanthropy. No need to complicate life by mixing the two. Well, one of the greatest revelations of my life was discovering that you can use your talents, passions, skills, and ability not only to earn an income but to make an impact and have an everlasting purpose. It was through that important discovery that business for impact became a core part of my brand identity.

STEPS TO BECOMING YOUR OWN CEO

There are three simple steps I like to follow when evaluating if I'm on the right track to being my own CEO:

- **Understand** who you were created to be.
- **Identify** your unique set of talents and skills.
- **Recognize** where God has planted you.

Understand who you were created to be. "We are His workmanship, created in Christ Jesus for good works, which God prepared beforehand that we should walk in them" (Ephesians 2:10 NKJV). God created us for His purposes, not our own. We were created in God's image, and our life's ultimate goal is to be in relationship with Him, to point others to Him, and to love and serve others along the way. But what's also so cool is that He created you with a unique purpose. He knew before you were even born the "good works" He prepared for you to do and how He would use them for His glory. I think there's something so empowering that the God of the universe has a specific plan for you and me to carry out. And He uses our gifts, talents, experiences, and even our messes to carry it out. That means you and I were created to join in God's rescue team, to walk boldly and obediently wherever He's calling us to go.

Identify your unique set of talents and skills. I think this part may be one of the toughest tasks in becoming your own CEO. We live in a culture that slaps labels on people and is constantly pressuring us to be, look, or act a certain way. It can make it hard to not only identify *who* you are, but also how to stand apart from the crowd. My good friend Dr. Leaf said, "You make a lousy someone else, but a fantastic you."[2] With the introduction of technology and social media, that pressure to be your label or fit in with everyone else has become that much greater. But God didn't create you to be everyone else. He created you to be *you*.

The best way I learn about myself and discover my abilities is through the process of elimination, or in simpler terms by trying something new. It sounds like it shouldn't be that simple. Too often, if something isn't complicated, it's not appreciated. We have this misconception that our life purpose must be connected to something rare or unconventional for it to be valuable. I believe that our life's purpose and calling can and most likely is directly related to things we enjoy, appreciate, resonate with, and are naturally good at. So go and try something new. It can be as simple as taking a painting class or signing up for a volunteer position, or as complicated as going on a mission trip in a country where nobody speaks your language.

Perhaps you'll discover that you have a unique ability to communicate well with people, or that you are able to solve problems others were stuck on. Maybe you'll learn that you are able to identify a flaw in the bookkeeping system and find ways to simplify it. Maybe you'll discover that you don't like being around people that much and you'd flourish working with statistics. Maybe your palate is brilliant in a kitchen, your mind fires up around design, or your heart beats for teaching kids. If you don't try, you'll never know what secret talents you might have.

Another way to discover your unique gifts or talents is by figuring out what brings you joy and identifying something others have pointed out in you or praised you for. You may have always loved bringing friends together, and your friends call you the "social chair," so your gift may be hospitality or loving on and welcoming others. Maybe you've always loved organizing or doing things behind the scenes to make things more efficient, so maybe your gift is in administration. Whatever that thing is, it's needed in the body of Christ.

Lastly, recognize where God has planted you. It's as simple as being aware of the opportunities right in front of you. Whether you're in a job you don't love, a city you're unhappy in, a lonely relationship, or just not where you thought you'd be, God has a purpose for you in it. I was stuck in a boarding school with nowhere else to go. Selling my cupcakes from under my bed was my only option, but that was also what made my little business work. It was the perfect setting for me to succeed. I didn't know it at the time, but it was a catalyst in discovering my passion for becoming an entrepreneur. It's always in hindsight that we see the plan laid out, isn't it?

That reminds me of a friend who made the decision to leave her job to pursue another one, only to feel she made a *huge* mistake. Haven't we all been there in one way or another? She cried for the first three months of her new job and was filled with doubt. She thought she'd prayed about it and had a peace about the decision, so why was she so miserable? Fast-forward two years, and she wouldn't have landed her "dream" job she went on to take if she hadn't taken that little job that made her miserable, because it was there that she learned all the skills needed to qualify for her current job.

I firmly believe God never wastes an experience, and He has you where you are for a reason. You may not be exactly where you hoped you'd be. But that doesn't mean you don't have a purpose exactly where God has planted you. Whether you feel you're in a dead-end job or a career lacking purpose, a stay-at-home mom wondering what meaning you can find in the mound of laundry you're folding, or still single after years of praying for a spouse, stop and look around. Chances are there is opportunity at every corner. Who in your world can you influence for good? What problems can you solve? You have no idea what hangs in the balance if you'd just be willing to be used, willing to show up where God has planted you right now.

CREATE A CEO MANUAL

No CEO can do their job well without some sort of guide or plan. They need guidelines and direction to help the company stay the course and ultimately reach their goals to success. As the CEO of Y.O.U., creating your own CEO manual is a must. In business, a manual contains the company's mission, vision, values, policies, processes, and standard operating procedures. A brand has a brand guideline that is used to make sure no one deviates from it. It contains logo usage, the brand color palette, the brand fonts, the brand voice, and even brand visuals. It's common for sports teams, especially football teams, to have some form of playbook. It's a document that contains their tactics, strategies, and game plan for the match ahead. In life, a manual, guideline, or playbook is a thorough plan that can help you establish clear expectations and achieve your intentions.

Grab a notebook or open your notes app on your phone and start establishing some of the most important information to include in your personal life manual:

1. Nonnegotiables

One of the most dangerous things we can do while trying to achieve our goals is to negotiate with ourselves. If you plan to work out today, then set a time, place, and routine, and do not give yourself permission to negotiate with yourself. If you do, the thirty-minute workout will easily turn into fifteen minutes, and the ten reps will turn into four. You might even feel like not working out at all. Workout nonnegotiables might seem silly, but I am a believer that we will attempt to do the big things in life the same way we attempt to do the small things. Establishing nonnegotiables—a set of principles, rules, values, or actions that we refuse to compromise on—helps us draw a moral and ethical line in the sand. I've had friends with nonnegotiables such as never eating lunch alone with a colleague of the opposite sex out of respect for their spouse, or not purchasing from a brand that supports causes they don't agree with.

An example of someone who stayed true to their nonnegotiables was Daniel in the Bible. As a young Israelite man, Daniel was part of a generation who was uprooted from their hometown and whisked away to Babylon by King Nebuchadnezzar in 586 BC. Once in Babylon, the king ordered the exiled Israelites to be immersed in Babylonian culture, customs, language, literature, food, and wine (Daniel 1:1–7). Now, this posed a major dilemma for Daniel. Learning the Chaldean language was one thing, but given his Jewish principles (particularly those concerning the consumption of kosher food), eating and drinking from the king's table was a major problem. According to Old Testament professor Dr. Stephen Miller, there were at least two factors that would have caused these Jews to be reluctant to eat the king's food:

- Much of the food at the king's court, like pork and horse-flesh, would have been considered unclean, either inherently or because the dishes were not prepared properly, according to the law of Moses.

- A portion of the meat and wine was (at least on occasions, if not always) first offered sacrificially to the Babylonian gods before being sent to the king; therefore, it would have been undesirable as it was associated with idolatrous worship.[3]

Talk about a culinary pickle! Would Daniel remain true to his Jewish convictions, or would he adapt his beliefs and fall in line with the rules of Babylonian society? We get the answer in Daniel 1:8: "But Daniel *resolved* not to defile himself with the royal food and wine, and he asked the chief official for permission not to defile himself this way" (emphasis added). Other versions translate *resolved* as "determined" (NLT), "made up his mind" (NASB), and "purposed in his heart" (NKJV). The point is that all these are in the past tense. Before Daniel was faced with the dilemma, he had already determined how he was going to respond. He had decided ahead of time that he was not going to negotiate. Like Daniel, what nonnegotiables do you have in place to remain faithful and honor God in potentially compromising situations?

2. Convictions

If nonnegotiables are your unwavering boundaries, then convictions are your *core beliefs that drive action and behavior.* Convictions are the why behind your nonnegotiables. Why you set them solidifies your decision to stick with them. When a decision comes along that might compromise one of your nonnegotiables, the convictions behind it are what will help you stand firm in the face of temptation. Some of my convictions include:

- All people were created in love, by love, and for love.
- As a believer, I am called to love God and love people.

- Be obedient to what God is calling me to do.
- Marriage is exclusive.
- The truth is exclusive.
- I have the power to choose who I allow to speak into my life.
- The Bible holds the only principles I live by.
- It is my job to care for and fuel my body with healthy nutrition.
- There is power in prayer.
- I am a colaborer with God.

As mentioned in Daniel's story, eating food that would "defile" him was nonnegotiable. His conviction, or the why behind his nonnegotiable, was that he believed three things: God exists and desired a personal relationship with him. God had given him (and the Israelites) specific commandments regarding dietary and purity laws for their own benefit. Commitment to such laws reflected a desire to honor, obey, serve, and love God.

Maybe you've never thought about defining your convictions. Here are some questions to get you thinking:

- What are some key issues that either stir your heart or rile you up?
- Do you have any heroes or role models whose actions and values inspire you? What do you admire most about them?
- How do you believe you should treat others, including classmates, teachers, and family members, and why are these behaviors important to you?

3. Mission and Vision Statement

Who doesn't love a cute new outfit? But what if that new outfit is not only ethically made but also gives individuals with disabilities the opportunity to show off their artistic abilities, earn an income, and continue to participate in art therapy classes?

Alivia, a women's fashion brand, stands out for turning stunning artwork from artists in art therapy into beautiful, wearable designs. What's cool is that every piece supports these artists financially and contributes to the art therapy program. Their mission is "to give purpose and voice to the previously unheard, showcasing the many talents and abilities of people with disabilities—and pushing the fashion industry further towards inclusivity."[4] It's like wearing art that tells a story and makes a real difference in people's lives. Cool, right?

Rooted in their mission statement is a direct effort to treat people right! And that's the beauty of it. A mission statement should provide clear direction for all who have bought into that mission. Do you have an established mission (in writing) that guides you in life? I have a few different mission statements for different areas in my life:

- **Faith:** "Take heart, be bold, and keep fighting for the one-more to know Jesus."
- **Marriage:** "Everyday all day, I choose you."
- **Business:** "To fuel and amplify faith, hope, and love."
- **Our Foundation:** "To bring faith, hope, and love to those needing a brighter day in their darkest hour of need."
- **Personal:** "To obediently and confidently walk in my God-given purpose and do all that I can with whatever I've got, wherever He has placed me."

If you don't have a mission statement yet, no worries! That's what this chapter is all about: *working to be your own CEO.* Here are some questions to work through as you draft your first mission statement:

- What core values and beliefs are most important to you?
- What do you aspire to achieve in the future?
- What are your passions and interests? What activities or causes do you feel most strongly about?
- What strengths, talents, or abilities do you possess that you want to use in pursuing your goals?
- How do you want to make a difference in your school, community, or world?

This exercise may seem overwhelming at first or too hard to imagine. But I encourage you to take it one step at a time. Doing the work, thinking it through, and writing out your personal mission statement will be a key factor in you seeing yourself as the CEO of *you*. Your mission statement will constantly point you back to your why and remind you of what makes *you* so special. When life changes and hardships or obstacles come your way, your mission statement will be like fuel in the car, like Google Maps on Bluetooth keeping you moving forward and on the right track.

4. Board of Directors

In most public companies, the CEO doesn't have full autonomy. They're accountable to a board of directors. I like to imagine the Trinity—Father, Son, and Holy Spirit—as the ultimate board of directors for our lives! As we take on the role of CEO, we quickly discover that we don't have full control over everything. That's perfectly okay! Just like a CEO seeks advice from their board for the best company decisions, we understand that our lives shine brightest when we acknowledge that God is the ultimate boss. He's got the wisdom, the game plan, and the big picture all figured out. So we happily surrender our need for total independence and realize that being accountable to God is the sweetest deal. Following His guidance is better than trying to call all the shots on our own. The reason we can trust God more than ourselves is because He can see the future clearly.

As you work through these four steps, creating your CEO manual will take time and require real work. You don't need to finish this in one day though. Your CEO manual should be deeply personal and will act as a great resource whenever you're faced with doubt or fear, hard decisions, unexpected circumstances, and new scenarios, reminding you of who you are and who you are called to be.

CAREER AS CALLING

In March 1888, British artist Lilias Trotter arrived in France at a time in Europe where the art world was exploding. Impressionism was on the rise, and artists like Claude Monet and Vincent van Gogh were all hard at work reimagining and redefining what beauty looked like. Conservative critics scoffed at their unconventional, sketch-like work while progressive writers praised them for challenging the artistic norm and painting "outside the box."

A decade earlier, when Lilias was an aspiring artist herself, she and her mom took a trip to Venice where they coincidentally met a man named John Ruskin. At the time, Ruskin was considered one of the most famous people in the English-speaking world.[5] He was a professor at Oxford and a highly respected art critic and philosopher. Knowing Ruskin's authority, Lilias's mother sent him a note with some of Lilias's sketches attached. Having seen hundreds of aspiring artists' work, Ruskin didn't expect much. But to his surprise, he saw incredible potential in Lilias. Her work was different, and he believed he could shape Lilias into one of the world's great watercolor artists. He even told Lilias that if she would devote herself, "she would be the greatest living painter in Europe and do things that would be immortal!"[6] Lilias began devoting herself to her art. However, while she was mentored by Ruskin, her heart was broken for the women in London. She started helping a local hostel that brought prostitutes in off the street, giving them a place to live, feel loved, and learn skills. She also opened a restaurant to serve hot meals to the poor.[7] As she served the women of London, her art took a back seat.

It was at this moment when Ruskin forced her to make a decision: her ministry or her art. She loved art, but she also cared for people. Imagine the internal agony! After much prayer and little sleep, she wrote to a friend saying, "I see clear as daylight now . . . I cannot dedicate myself to painting in the way that [Ruskin] means and continue to seek first the kingdom of God and his righteousness."[8] Lilias made up her mind, so when she found herself in France in March 1888, it wasn't to meet up with the van Goghs of the world. It was to board a train. To leave behind fame and pursue her calling: to serve the least of these, specifically in Algeria. After being rejected by the North African mission board (because they feared she wouldn't be able to endure harsh desert conditions), Lilias decided to go to Algeria anyway, using her own resources to get there.

Lilias arrived in Algeria alone, with no friends and no knowledge of the Arabic language. Despite her lack of training and connections, her deep faith, willingness, and prayers led her to serve the Algerian people for forty years. She revolutionized missions by using art to paint the gospel and pioneered "wordless evangelism." Amazing, right? When Lilias had to make the tough choice between her two loves, art or people, Ruskin asked her to choose one. But God instructed her to choose both. She could've chosen a career as an artist, and who knows what she would've accomplished, but instead she chose her calling, where she lived fully into her art and her faith.

Be inspired to embark on your own mission to discover your vision for your life. Learn how to distinguish your unique traits and skills from what society or culture tells you they should be. Stretch your limits and stop confining your potential to a label someone else has put on you. God's identity for you is much bigger and bolder than what anyone can give you.

Cultivating growth for kingdom impact requires work. Planting encompasses processing your past in a healthy way, finding meaning in your story, and sharing what you've learned with others. When you do the hard work of planting new seeds of perspective, goal setting, and identity building, you move closer to living out who God has created you to be.

CHECKLIST

My hope in Part 2 of this book is for you to:

- Reframe your idea of failure.
- Learn how to distinguish your unique traits and skills from what culture tells you they should be.
- Recognize the people and places God has put you in proximity with.
- Understand the connection between career and calling.
- Be inspired to embark on your own mission to discover your vision for your life.

RECAP

In chapter 4, you learned that a setback is a setup for a success story. Taking a risk and starting a new chapter in life often requires several starts. Believe it or not, failure is a key ingredient in success. Choosing to continue to come back after challenges knock you down strengthens your character and your faith. I shared in chapter 5 one of the most empowering statements that has changed my life: "You are your own CEO." Knowing and growing your brand identity entails recognizing and implementing your personal non-negotiables, principles, passions, and what you want to be known for in a kingdom-driven direction. Living this out means understanding whose you were created to be, identifying your God-given talents, and recognizing where God has planted you.

THE BIG PICTURE

Most of us like a good comeback story. I know I do! Seeing someone choose not to let a setback have the final word in his or her life inspires and motivates us. It makes us believe anything is possible. If you're into sports, you know that the return of Michael Jordan into the basketball league in 1995 after announcing his retirement was a huge comeback. After not playing for a year and a half, he continued to dominate on the court. Think of actors like Brendan Fraser and Jennifer Coolidge whose careers were on pause for different reasons, and years later their reentry into the acting world showcased breathtaking and award-winning performances. How about Steve Jobs and Apple? After the company fired Jobs in 1985, Apple plummeted into a downward spiral. When Jobs returned in 1997, he revived the company and built the tech giant to what it is today.

You may have a comeback story of your own or have drawn inspiration from one. While setbacks are never fun, these obstacles in life do not signify the end of the journey. If you choose to view yourself as a coworker with God in His story you can ask Him to help you find meaning in your setbacks, partner with Him through your next steps, and find joy in knowing you are beloved no matter how real the obstacles you're facing or the odds that are stacked against you. It starts in the mind.

Building a powerful mindset is the antidote to falling into the temptation to quit trying and to give in to frustration and despair after you failed the test, the relationship ended, the job fell through, or your idea flopped. Rejections, detours, and unforeseen twists are as much a part of the process as celebrating wins. When we choose to use the lows not as stopping points but as stepping stones, a world of possibility opens. We become stronger. We build our faith muscles. We bolster our character. We learn to rely on the Lord and not our own strength. And we listen more carefully to where He's leading us next.

Comebacks are possible. Why? Because we are not alone. God is with us every step of the way. His presence, love, mercy, and grace remain steady and secure even when our circumstances change.

Best of all, we can champion our comebacks because His Son Jesus ushered in the biggest comeback in all of history when He conquered death and rose again.

Regardless of the feelings of doubt, insecurity, inadequacy, or uncertainty you may wrestle with, knowing that you are a child of God and lining up your priorities, your focus, and your future with His eternal kingdom in mind is a mental game-changer. When you are synched with the Creator of this universe, no matter what happens, you can be confident knowing He will use everything for a good purpose. Believing in this truth is vital to fully engaging in life and living out your purpose using the unique skills and talents you were born with.

READ, REFLECT, AND ANSWER

Are you feeling crushed by a setback right now? What is it? Name it and let's bring it to the Lord:

What is one thing you've learned in this section about how God sees you? Name it and write it below:

Read Philippians 1:3–11. Imagine this is Jesus talking to you after you've suffered a bad setback:

> I thank my God every time I remember you. In all my prayers for all of you, I always pray with joy because of your partnership in the gospel from the first day until now, being confident of this, that he who began a good work in you will carry it on to completion until the day of Christ Jesus.
>
> It is right for me to feel this way about all of you, since I have you in my heart and, whether I am in chains or defending and confirming the gospel, all of you share in God's grace with me. God can testify how I long for all of you with the affection of Christ Jesus.
>
> And this is my prayer: that your love may abound more and more in knowledge and depth of insight, so that you may be able to discern what is best and may be pure and blameless for the day of Christ, filled with the fruit of righteousness that comes through Jesus Christ—to the glory and praise of God.

Underline the sentences that encouraged you the most in this verse.

When I handed over my crown as Miss Universe, it felt like I'd handed over my identity, including my purpose and my meaning. It was a hard but significant lesson for me. When you discover that no thing or person can ever take away your identity as a daughter of God, you can live the truth of Ephesians 2:10, that we are God's "workmanship, created in Christ Jesus for good works, which God prepared beforehand so that we would walk in them" (NASB1995).

In chapter 5, I wrote:

> I didn't realize it at the time, but that "different" I was searching for was my *eternal identity.* Discovering the desire for a deeper

purpose, knowing that my life had more meaning than just making money for a brand I realized that you can't take charge of your life or define your brand identity if you don't understand who you were created to be and the plan your Creator has for you.

What are three ways that an eternal identity is more significant than an identity based on performance, looks, wins, or social status?

1.

2.

3.

List three ways you can build your personal brand the kingdom way. For example, you can define success as obedience to what Christ has asked of you rather than by the number of likes or followers or shares.

1.

2.

3.

ACCEPT THE CHALLENGE

One of the most fundamental ways to plant seeds of new values, habits, and perspectives that align with a sustainable and fulfilling identity is to create a personal mission statement, a set of nonnegotiables, and a list of convictions as well as establish a board of directors. Hey, you're the CEO, remember? Right now, I'd like you to spend time creating your own. I've unpacked these three things in chapter 5. You can refer back for more detailed explanations of each item.

PERSONAL MISSION STATEMENT

A mission statement helps us understand our purpose and why we do what we do. My personal mission statement is

> to obediently and confidently walk in my God-given purpose to do all that I can with whatever I've got, wherever He has placed me.

Your turn: My Personal Mission Statement is:

NONNEGOTIABLES

Nonnegotiables are a set of principles, rules, values, or actions that we refuse to compromise on. One example is "I will read my Bible every day." Or, "I will not get involved in romantic relationships with anyone who is not a follower of Jesus."

Your turn: My Nonnegotiables are:

CONVICTIONS

Convictions are synonymous with core values and reflect the why behind your nonnegotiables. They drive your behaviors and your actions. Some of mine include: "As a believer I am called to love God and love people." And, "God calls me to be obedient in all I do."

Your turn: My convictions are:

BOARD OF DIRECTORS

Finally, there's nothing you have to draft here, only remember. Never forget that while you may be the CEO of your life, God is your board of directors. You answer to Him alone and always.

PRAYER

(Read this prayer out loud in closing)

> Thank You God that as Your daughter, I can ride life's highs and lows. No matter the outcome of situations, I can trust that You have my best interest in mind. Unlock in me the revelation of what it means to be Your child so I can live fully and successfully. In Jesus' name, amen.

PART THREE

GROW

I will bless the LORD *at all times;*
his praise will always be on my lips.
I will boast in the LORD*;*
the humble will hear and be glad.

PSALM 34:1–2 (CSB)

Have you ever repotted a plant? You take it out of the smaller pot, gently loosen its roots, and place it in a bigger pot for it to stretch out and grow. Depending on the size of the plant, it's essential to repot for the sake of the plant's health. I'm no master gardener, but in life I do feel like we experience these types of "repotting" seasons. Times when we've experienced the pain of being uprooted, confused about how things would shake out, but in the end, we look back and see how each repotting moment was necessary for our growth as individuals. That's how I felt writing chapters 6, 7, and 8.

In this Grow section, I share some of the hardest and most stretching moments of my life. Although they were difficult to navigate, I learned the reality that God works all things together for good! These chapters offer my personal insights on transforming pain into purpose, choosing compassion over convenience, and finding a sense of belonging as we continue to grow into the purposeful individuals we were created to be. In this section, my hope is that you're going to:

- Understand that God can use our trials in life for His triumph.
- Address any untouched trauma and begin taking steps toward healing.
- Realize the power of your story and your voice.
- Be challenged to seek out and act obediently on opportunities to love and serve others well.
- Find freedom in eliminating comparison and understand the importance of building a strong community.

SIX

PAIN TO PURPOSE

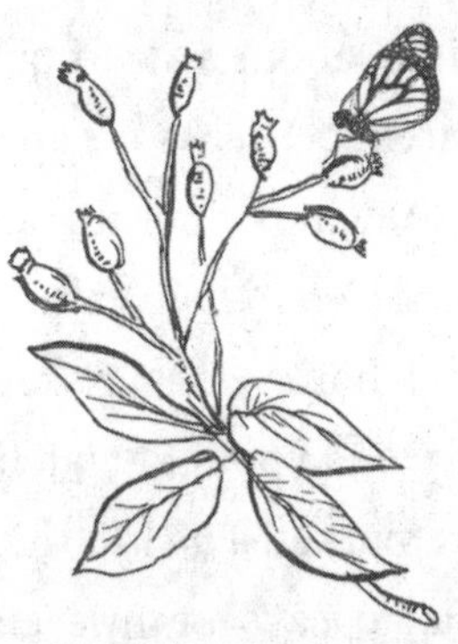

WARNING

This chapter contains several traumatic stories of violence that may be triggering. My hope is that in sharing these stories, you would find hope where you need it, know you are not alone, and believe that healing is possible.

On a Wednesday afternoon in June 2017, I was running late to an event I had committed to months in advance as part of my Miss South Africa calendar. I had been excited about it for weeks. The event was supposed to be a fun and memorable night. But a forest fire had broken out deep in the mountains outside of Sedgefield, my hometown, close to the neighboring town of Knysna. The fires had been bulldozing everything in their way for a week at that point and were getting more powerful and dangerous by the hour due to the dried-out vegetation after months of drought and rising gale-force winds. It had been one of those "it won't happen to me" situations—and then our town was asked to evacuate.

As part of my Miss South Africa contract, I was living in Johannesburg at the time, about a two-hour flight away from my hometown and my parents. I felt so helpless in that moment. I couldn't even be there to help my mom and stepdad grab the bare necessities, pack the car, or keep them calm. It was an awful feeling. Every person I knew back home was at risk, from my middle school teacher to the sweet lady who I bought Nutella pancakes from every Saturday at the farmers market. The last thing my mom said to me on the phone before I had to leave for my event was, "If they don't get the fires under control, our whole town could burn to the ground."

I grabbed my handbag, threw my phone inside, and downed a cup of cold coffee to hopefully get a little caffeine kick before my event. The Miss South Africa organization had been extremely supportive, and it was ultimately my decision to follow through and attend even though I was worried sick. My parents had instilled a deep sense of responsibility in me from a young age, so I wasn't going to bail. Plus, it was supposed to be a quick and easy event; I should be back home in just over an hour.

While holding my keys, bag, and empty cup, I hopped toward the front door as I tried putting on and adjusting the straps around my ankles attached to six-inch platform heels that matched my black cocktail dress. The little black dress my stylist had dropped off earlier that day was decorated with small ostrich feathers and a ton of sequins, and was designed by one of my favorite South African designers, Anel Botha. Just before I stepped out of my apartment, I felt a prompting to take off my big diamond look-alike earrings and ran back to my room to replace them with smaller, less flashy studs. Of course, I couldn't find the back of one earring! At that point, I was fully running late and feeling even more flustered on top of being stressed and anxious about the situation in my hometown. I couldn't be bothered to do up the top few buttons at the back of my dress as I ran out the front door and carefully down the staircase.

As I jumped in the driver's seat of my new car, which was from the Miss South Africa prize package, I quickly realized I was about to drive this manual transmission car in six-inch heels because there wasn't time to take those bad boys off.

"I've got this," I told myself.

If you're wondering what a manual transmission is, let me enlighten you. Basically, if an automatic vehicle is a Nespresso machine where you just press one button and get a delicious cup of coffee, then a manual transmission car is like a French press where you have to grind the beans by hand, then boil water on the gas stove. If you don't know what a French press is, then it's not just my ten-year high school reunion last year that's making me feel old right now.

Anyway, I successfully maneuvered the gas and clutch, switched from first to second gear, and made my way into rush-hour traffic, but I was cutting it close. Thankfully, the event was only a mile or so up the road. Just as I was approaching the event's parking garage, the traffic light turned red. I was about four cars from the front when I noticed three suspicious men on the left side of my vehicle walking toward me. At first I didn't make much of the situation because in South Africa during peak hour traffic, it was pretty common for vendors to sell goods, for commuters to get in and out of minibus taxis, and for pedestrians to braid through the slow-moving traffic to catch a lift. However, I had a strong feeling that the three men on my left were not vendors, commuters, or pedestrians. Instead, they walked with their heads down like they were on a mission.

When I looked to my right, I realized what was happening. I spotted a fourth man about three lanes away who was also walking toward my car. Based on what I'd learned in driving safety courses, seeing the man on my right confirmed my suspicions; I was being surrounded and set up for a carjacking. There have been many moments that have molded me into the woman I am today, but the events that followed drastically shaped my life.

Praying for the traffic light to turn green, I started looking for a way out in case this became the worst-case scenario. I was blocked in by a steel barrier on the side of the road and bumper-to-bumper traffic all around me. I had nowhere to go, and the traffic light felt like it was stuck on red. The man on my right reached the car first. I didn't get a good look at him because I was trying not to make eye contact.

He knocked on my driver's side window. I briefly glanced over at him, hoping to see that he was trying to sell me a beaded flower, a drink, or even fresh fruit. He wasn't. He knocked on my window a second time, so I glanced over again. By then, the three men on the left had reached me too. One of them leaned over the front of the car and pointed a gun through the windshield at my head. I was surrounded. There was one man per door. They yanked and pulled at my car doors, but my doors were locked. The traffic light was still red, so I couldn't speed away.

With a gun aimed at my head and the horror stories of similar situations flashing through my mind, I realized I had no choice but to surrender my vehicle and belongings. I put my hands up in the air, kept my head down, and focused on not making eye contact, just like I'd been taught in self-defense and safety driving courses. I remembered to comply, to not make a scene, and to not engage in any sudden movements. I slowly opened my door and started sliding out of my car. Thankfully, it had a safety feature that was activated, which only allowed for the driver's door to be unlocked instead of all the doors once the door handle was pulled open. With one foot after the other, I slowly got out of the car, my hands in the air holding my phone in one hand. Once again, I was blocked in between the open car door and the man on my right. There was no space to run away. He snatched my phone out of my hand and started patting me down. In just my cocktail dress, high heels, and (thankfully!) no flashy jewelry, I didn't have anything else on me for him to take. Relieved, I thought, *It's okay, Demi. He probably just wants your belongings. He has your phone. He'll let you go now.*

Time was not on my side. I didn't have the luxury of formulating a strategy to get out of the situation. Nor could I dial the police on my phone that he'd just taken from me. I did the best thing I could think of in that moment and tried to make a run for it. But he grabbed me by my wrist and pulled me back toward the car and growled, "You're going with us." Suddenly, a core lesson from the self-defense workshop flashed through my mind: "Never go to the second destination! Whatever is about to happen in broad daylight and peak traffic will most likely not get any better down some dark alley."

That's when I decided to fight back. I made peace with the fact that I might get shot, but in that moment it was better than agreeing to go with them. I had to act—fast. I needed to buy myself a small window of opportunity to get away before the other three men, still surrounding the car, could get around to overpower me.

I remembered one important self-defense tactic: go for the throat! Adrenaline burst through me, and I used that swell of energy to punch him right in the throat. *Boom!* It was by no means a great punch. I didn't do much damage, but it was enough to startle him, make him let go of my arm, and buy me a split second to run away.

I ran right up that busy dual-carriage-lane road in my six-inch heels. The cars surrounding me at the traffic light started moving again as I ran toward the intersection in front of me. All I could think of in that moment was to get as far away from my attackers as possible. Lights flashed. Horns blared. My heart raced. The fact that I didn't get hit by another car was a miracle. I crossed a few lanes trying to use the traffic to create a barrier between my carjackers and me.

Should I stop to take the shoes off so that I can run faster? No, absolutely not! There is no time. Suck it up and keep going. Just keep going! As I ran in between the traffic, my second instinct was to ask for help. I knocked on as many car windows as possible. Some cars had men in them; others had groups of women. I noticed families, people driving alone, a group of young men, and older folks, yet not one single person would stop for me. The astonishing part was that I looked many people in the eye through their slightly open car windows, and they could hear what I was saying. They could hear the desperation in my voice and see the tears of pure panic rolling down my cheeks. This was truly the most terrifying part of the whole ordeal—not a single soul would help me. I had no idea what would happen next.

As I ran up the avenue, I kept looking over my shoulder to see if I was being chased, wondering when I would hear the blast of a gunshot or feel a bullet pierce my back. The men hadn't driven off in my car yet, which made me wonder if they were after me instead of my car. Approaching the traffic light at the big intersection, I had no idea how I could safely cross the road. It was winter in South Africa, so the sun sets earlier, and I knew that if someone didn't help me quickly, I was soon going to be left on that street in the dark. I suddenly remembered a gas station a mile or two down that road. It would be my best next option since nobody was stopping for me. Fear and panic knotted my insides. I wasn't sure who I could trust. I thought that maybe the armed men might have other people working with them, waiting in a random car, or even at that gas station, who could snatch me up and take me God knows where. Any car that whizzed by might be their getaway car. The sky darkened by the second. I didn't have many options, so I decided to keep trying my luck and continue knocking on a few more car windows as I ran to beg for someone to let me in.

I vividly remember asking one specific woman through her cracked open window, "Please help me! I just got carjacked!" She shook her head and waved her hands, signaling for me to leave her alone as she rolled up her window. "Get away," she yelled as if I were the criminal. My heart sank. This was hopeless. Nobody was willing to help. Nobody was willing to be interrupted. Nobody wanted to put themselves at risk. Part of me didn't blame them; I understood. South Africa has staggering crime statistics. I'd grown up dreading this moment. My feet felt numb, and my heart raced as taillights kept flashing past me. Just then, on the opposite side of the road, two beams of light from a tiny car swerved over to the side. The screeching brakes echoed in my ears.

The driver yelled at me. Finally, someone was willing to help! I looked left and right and then crossed the road one more time. Her little car was old and looked pretty beat up. I could tell that she was very young but clearly very brave. "Get in! Get in!" she yelled at me. Just before she leaned over to unlock and open the little car door, she looked at me and asked, "You don't have a gun, right?" "No," I insisted. "I was just carjacked!" She let me into her car and sped off, taking the first turn she could, then a second, then a third, making sure that if someone was following us, we would have lost them.

I asked the young woman to take me to the event I felt like I'd left for hours earlier, though it had only been about twenty minutes. I knew that there would be staff there who could help me. That courageous and sweet young lady, who I later found out was only nineteen years old, dropped me off at the event venue. I reached down and ripped the stilts off my feet, then ran through the shopping mall, down the escalator, and to the storefront that was hosting the event. Out of breath, I asked for someone to go and get my Miss South Africa team.

A few of my team members came running, called the nearest police station when they heard what happened, and found the security from the shopping mall where the event was being hosted. We walked out into the enclosed parking lot where, unbelievably, you could actually see the spot where I was carjacked through the security fencing. I pointed my car out. It was right where I had left it. Even though the spot was so close to the event, my instinct had been to run in the opposite direction because the carjackers were blocking my entrance to the venue. When we got back to my car, I was stunned to learn that two off-duty private security guards had been on their way home in a minibus taxi that was behind me when the carjacking occurred. When they saw what happened, they confronted my attackers after I'd run away. They weren't wearing bulletproof vests or carrying any kind of protection with them, but they managed to retrieve my handbag with my wallet, identity documents, and some personal items from the carjackers. At the time, I got their information and the company they worked for, but in the chaos of the rest of the night, I somehow lost it. I'm still sad about it because I never got to thank them.

It turned into a long night of police reports, waiting for the forensics team to come and take fingerprints from the car and trying to check in with my parents. To add more stress to the already unfortunate evening, the signal towers around my hometown caught on fire shortly after I called my mom. I couldn't reach her again until the next day but was relieved to learn that she was okay—and Sedgefield was okay too. I was emotionally drained and physically exhausted from all the adrenaline. I booked myself into a hotel room as the carjackers still had my apartment keys. With my dirty, bare feet, raccoon eyes from mascara tears, and a scratchy sequined dress, I entered my hotel room and threw down the few items I had grabbed from my apartment. I didn't know what to do next. I was hungry from all the adrenaline and emotion but too nauseous from the shock to eat. It felt like a big frog had gotten lodged in my throat, and I couldn't get a breath. I walked around my hotel room, checking that every window was locked. I proceeded to try and scrub away what had just happened, but not before barricading my door with a chair and locking myself in the bathroom.

A FEAR-FILLED FUTURE

I stayed in that hotel for close to a week while my locks were changed. When I moved back into my apartment, I was changed too. Statistics tell us that approximately 736 million women worldwide have been subjected to physical and/or sexual violence at least once in their lives,[1] so I know I'm not alone in how my body processed the trauma of what I'd been through. It was hard to fall asleep at night. Any little peep or squeak made the hairs on the back of my neck stand up. I couldn't close my eyes while taking a shower or washing my hair because I was terrified that I wouldn't hear if somebody broke into my apartment when the water was running.

The fact that the carjackers had gotten away with my cell phone and a remote to open my apartment building's security gate was a horrifying thought. I barely slept for the next few weeks. The sleep deprivation left me even more anxious and on edge. I started over-analyzing everything. *Was that creak a floorboard or an intruder? Was that person staring at me one of my carjackers?* I left my car in the mall parking lot where the incident occurred because driving it home was too triggering. I relied on a car service and friends to drive me around for a week or two until I eventually mustered up the courage to bring my car home. It took me a good month to get comfortable enough to get back into that car alone. I avoided peak-hour traffic like the plague. I deliberately scheduled appointments around it. I got up at 4:00 a.m. to go to the gym so that I could work out, get back home, and get ready for my day all while avoiding traffic.

These anxiety-ridden habits continued for weeks. There were days I just wanted to stay in bed, eat ice cream, and watch a TV show to escape the reality of what I'd lived through that night. Other days I just had to put my big girl panties on and do what I needed to do to get through the day, even if that meant masking my constant anxiety and fear. I was leaving to compete for Miss Universe in three months, and I didn't have time to stop or slow down.

IT'S NOT OUR FAULT

For a long time, I felt like the carjacking was somehow my fault; that I did something to bring that on myself. Operating from a victim mentality, I blamed myself for being an easy target by being too dressed up or by making the wrong decision to drive in rush-hour traffic. At first, I didn't want anyone besides my loved ones to know what had happened because it made me feel so weak.

I needed to blame someone, and the easiest person to blame was me. It took some time for me to realize that wasn't true. After talking it through with my stepmom, who is a neuropsychologist, she taught me that blaming yourself in situations like this is a common response to trauma. It really comes down to self-protection and control. Blaming yourself can give you a sense of control, even if that sense of control is misplaced. If you say something is your fault, it makes you feel like you could prevent a similar situation from happening in the future. Admitting something was out of your control leaves you feeling helpless and vulnerable. Oftentimes, blaming yourself feels safer than realizing and admitting that the trauma that happened to you was outside of your control entirely.

Today, I can talk about the carjacking without feeling overwhelmed, but it has not been an easy road to get to a place of healing. It took time, patience, willingness, strength, and a good amount of trauma counseling to heal from the damage this incident caused.

I have learned that a negative experience can feel personal, all-encompassing, and permanent, especially if you are not in a healthy state of mind. It can lead your mind to believe that it will definitely happen to you again, even if there is nothing indicating that this is the case. I felt this way after my carjacking, like my perpetrators had specifically selected me. I didn't want to drive myself anywhere because I thought they were waiting for me around the next corner. Eventually, I learned that I had to change my mindset. Even though I was a carjacking victim once, I didn't need to stay a victim to the unhealthy thought patterns long term.

My stepmom helped me realize that true healing won't start until you acknowledge that you actually have a problem—in my case, acute stress disorder (ASD). Over time I've learned this is a normal and transient reaction to trauma. It lasts for approximately thirty days. If things don't get better, that's when it progresses into PTSD, post-traumatic stress disorder. Interestingly, psychological debriefing about your trauma within seventy-two hours has a significant impact on preventing ASD from progressing to PTSD. Asking and genuinely accepting help was one of the most difficult yet powerful choices that contributed to my healing process. When you start healing by getting professional help from someone who can equip you with the tools and skills you need to adjust your thought patterns, you start realizing that the trauma you went through was not your fault; unfortunately, it could have happened to anyone. Therapy helped me realize this terrible event would not happen to me every time I left the house. Eventually, I started trusting that I wouldn't be scarred permanently.

I attended EMDR (Eye Movement Desensitization and Reprocessing) therapy, a wonderful technique that helped me remove the fear from the facts. I was able to unlock some of the memories that I had suppressed, which gave me the ability to talk about what happened. Very simply put, think middle school biology class. The brain consists of two sides: the logical, analytical side and the more creative and emotional side. In order to process anything that's happened to us, we need to think about the event logically and analytically, but we also need to be creative to think of a solution. Furthermore, we need to take our emotions into account; otherwise, we get to the place where we say, "My head says this, but my heart says that."

If our head (the logical, analytical side) and our heart (the feelings side) are not on the same page, we haven't processed an experience in full. Talk therapy assists in integrating these two sides with each other. So I spoke about the carjacking as much as possible, and eventually I stopped reliving the event every time I talked about it. I stopped smelling my attacker's sweaty hoodie and no longer felt his rough hands grabbing my wrist when I told the story. The event became a part of my life's story instead of the story defining my life.

The small, healthy steps I took (like being honest with myself and others) resulted in big progress. I eventually gained the courage to drive up the avenue where the carjacking took place on my way to the gym instead of taking another route. It took a great deal of courage to move back into my apartment once my locks were changed. I tried to be kind to myself and gave myself permission to call a friend or family member at any point in the day so I would not feel alone. I would leave my phone on speaker while I got ready or cooked my food, not because I needed a conversation but because I found comfort in just knowing someone was with me.

It was so important for me to be kind to myself on the road to mental and emotional healing. Professional counseling played a pivotal part in my healing process. If you are currently experiencing the emotional effects of a traumatic situation, I want to encourage you to seek help. I know it can be hard to reach out, but trauma is not meant to be left untreated. Shoving it into a box in your mind doesn't mean it stops affecting you. Most countries have free counseling services, and you can also find faith-based counseling options through most local churches.

FINDING STRENGTH IN NUMBERS

The night after my carjacking, I slept with one eye open for what felt like three minutes before waking up the next morning to get to my 6:00 a.m. radio show appearance. I mentioned earlier that I do not like to cancel a commitment, and I meant it. I didn't think twice about showing up to the radio show as that commitment was bigger than just myself. We had set up the interview a few days earlier when the news broke of the devastating fires. My goal was to use the platform I'd gained as Miss South Africa to raise support for the hundreds of families in the region where I grew up whose livelihoods had been destroyed. I was still processing everything that had happened less than twelve hours prior while trying to hold it together on a national radio show. I was struggling to not lose focus on why I was there—to support people in desperate need. We managed to raise R821 894.00 (around $40,000) in less than an hour, which funded local nonprofits in helping rebuild the lives of families who had lost everything. It was such an honor to be able to use my platform to give back to others.

That wasn't the only outcome that day though. During the radio show, people caught on to the breaking news story: "Miss South Africa carjacked." As Miss South Africa, I'd always felt like I was supposed to be the strong and perfect "big sister figure" for other girls, and the carjacking incident left me feeling like I'd somehow failed in my role and would be seen as weak. What followed taught me that the most unexpected and sometimes ugliest situations in our life can lead to finding our biggest purpose and calling.

Before the interview wrapped up, I was asked on live radio about what had happened the night before. At first, I was too scared to answer. I felt uncomfortable, unsure of what to say. But I fumbled my way through sharing the trauma I hadn't even begun to process yet. Though I showed up for that radio interview to help others, God showed up to help me!

When I got back to my hotel after the interview, I realized that my social media was blowing up. I expected the worst. I opened Instagram and saw thousands of messages. Barely looking at the screen out of fear, terrified that my story may have somehow been misinterpreted, I clicked on the first message, then the second, third, tenth, twentieth. Women from all over the country were pouring out their stories to me. They had heard my radio interview and were sharing how something similar had happened to them. Many women and young girls mentioned how they'd felt like a weak target, incapable of standing up for themselves, not just in a carjacking situation, but in everyday life.

I was not alone. We were not alone. I gained a sisterhood of strangers I never knew I needed. That interview became a connection point for all of us. I couldn't have imagined all the ways God would use the most painful event in my life. I'm so grateful that I was able to escape that carjack situation, but it also opened my eyes and broke my heart for the many women around the world who have not been able to get away from their painful reality. Because of their stories and my own experience, I started educating myself on the overwhelming statistics on violence against women and children. I started to learn more about all the people in the world who didn't have a voice, who didn't feel safe, who felt helpless, and I wanted to do something about it. God used my trauma and turned it into one of my life's greatest purposes: fighting for those who can't fight for themselves, being a voice for the voiceless, and empowering women all over the world to break barriers and overcome challenges with confidence.

Out of my most traumatic experience, Unbreakable was born. It birthed in me a passion to find a way to make the practical tools and skills I had learned through self-defense and safety driving courses accessible to woman all over South Africa. More importantly, my heart was so broken for each and every woman who told me that they didn't feel worthy of a loving relationship, that they didn't have the confidence to leave a violent relationship because their partner paid their rent, or that they'd never had the courage to share their story with anyone because they blamed themselves for what had happened to them. I realized that we had more in common than we probably ever knew. The most significant truth I realized was that alone we can be strong, but together, arm in arm, we can be *Unbreakable*.

God used that mess of a night and turned it into one of my life's greatest messages. He transformed me from not being able to close my eyes in the shower to standing in front of hundreds of women sharing my story. The Unbreakable workshops put lifesaving skills and mindsets into the hands of hundreds of women, with the help of field experts. I realized that as individuals we might be left emotionally hurt, bruised, traumatized, scared, or insecure from a situation, but when we stand in unity, speak up for someone who can't speak up for themselves, or simply show up for someone in need, we can be less lonely, less vulnerable, and . . . unbreakable. Think about a stressful situation you dealt with and the relief you felt when you got to share it with a friend and realized that they have been through something similar. Didn't it feel like you were able to throw off the forty-pound bag of sand you'd been carrying on your shoulders and you were finally able to take a deep breath?

One of the sweetest rewards is witnessing how sharing your own story can light a spark in someone else to do the same, and in so doing they can also break barriers and overcome challenges. A young lady approached me after an Unbreakable workshop one day and told me that hearing other women boldly speak up enabled her to find the courage to file a police report for the first time. I recently received a comment from a young lady on social media who attended one of the first Unbreakable workshops in 2017, sharing how it impacted her so greatly that she still applies the skills she learned that day to her everyday life. The nineteen-year-old girl who stopped to help me that day was the catalyst to the birth of Unbreakable. It's a daily reminder to never doubt the ripple effect of goodness that can stem from a single act of courageous kindness.

FROM VICTIM TO VOICE

As a result of what Unbreakable snowballed into, I have had the honor of working with nonprofit organizations around the world, including the Tim Tebow Foundation founded by my husband. I am not only able to serve alongside my husband, but I have had the honor of meeting and getting to know some of whom I believe are the most courageous and resilient women in the world. There is one specific lady who holds a very special place in my heart and whose story encapsulates the term "pain to purpose" so powerfully. Her name is Mimi, and she gives the best hugs. Even though we do not live in the same country or speak a similar language, her life has been a great encouragement and inspiration to me.

Mimi was trapped in the evil cycle of human trafficking for years. One awful night, Mimi was sold to a cannibal. Yes, a literal cannibal. Once she realized his intentions, she did everything to escape. Mimi hid in a banana plantation all through the night, and at the break of dawn, she searched for help. Thankfully, there was someone who cared enough to lend a helping hand. This led to a path of Mimi being brought into a long-term restoration program that provided her a safe place to close her eyes in peace where she was protected from her perpetrators.

She received in-depth counseling in a space where she could rest and experience physical and emotional healing. As Mimi made progress, she was able to learn basic life skills, setting her up for independence. Today, Mimi is not just a survivor on the safe campus where she was first identified as a victim; she is a thriver! She has chosen to be a leader on the safe campus, and her story has allowed her to serve dozens of women who have come after her by being able to resonate and understand their pain on a deeper level than anyone else can. Mimi also discovered a skill for hairdressing and is now teaching women in her community how to use that skill to help create independence for themselves by earning a sustainable income (talk about passing the torch!).

Just as someone shared Mimi's story with me, bringing me

hope, have you ever found hope or healing when someone shared their story with you? I don't think our life's calling and purpose is completely unrelated to our personal stories and experiences. I believe our personal experiences become our purpose because we've walked in those shoes and have come out on the other side, able to tell the story.

It reminds me of a Japanese artform called *kintsugi*, which is the process of repairing broken pottery by filling in the cracks with gold. Even though the cracks become more visible than before, they are now beautiful. The cracks are no longer the flaws; they have become what makes the restored pottery a masterpiece. This artform transforms a broken piece of pottery, no longer fit for use, and makes it whole again. Now it's not only fit for use; it's also more valuable and beautiful than it ever was before. I believe that's what God wants to do with all our broken pieces. He takes our personal experiences (the trials and trauma) and refines and reshapes us, taking all the broken pieces and making us whole again. But not just whole. Through healing we become stronger, more valuable, and more beautiful than ever before. We can begin to reframe our hardships and brokenness as a catalyst for growth, making us into the women we are today. When we see our trauma and our pain through that lens, and we're able to start sharing our stories with other women, we go from feeling broken to becoming unbreakable.

SEVEN

BE *THAT GIRL*

WARNING

This chapter shares a heartbreaking story that includes domestic sexual abuse. My heart in sharing this story is not for it to be traumatizing or hurtful, but to shed light on the horrific reality that many experience. My hope in sharing this reality is to encourage conversation between us as a community and hopefully between families so that we can call out the wrongs committed and show up to be a helping hand in unjust situations.

Yes, you read the title of this chapter right. Be *that girl.* No, I am not confused. And no, I didn't mean to write "Don't be *that girl.*" When you hear the phrase "that girl," do you think about the girl who is always causing a scene? The one who bats her eyelashes and flirts to get her way, the girl who always responds with a passive-aggressive one-liner, the one who makes everyone look bad to make themselves feel better? The "pick me" girl, the teacher's pet? I know you know her. If you don't, then you at least know of her. Maybe you're reading this wondering if you've ever been her.

Ooh, that's a hard pill to swallow. But if it makes you feel any better, I have certainly been the teacher's pet a few times too many. I couldn't do a thing wrong in school. My homework was always done, and if it wasn't, my teachers would turn a blind eye because I never caused trouble. I played sports, said the right things, did the right things, wore the right things, and made the other kids in my class furious, especially the girls, because I refused to go with the flow no matter how much frustration it caused the rest of my class.

Thankfully, looking back on our immaturity and recognizing how we could have done better is what growing up is all about. Experiencing the eye-rolling frustration and even anger "that girl" unlocks in us should inspire us to never want to be the girl who frustrates, angers, annoys, or irritates others. I know I've been challenged to be more forgiving, loving, kind, gentle, encouraging, thoughtful, and brave. *That's* the kind of girl I want to be. It took a frightening experience for me to recognize the power of being the other kind of *that girl*—let me introduce you to her.

WILLING TO BE INTERRUPTED

You might think the most traumatic part of my carjacking story was having a gun pointed at my head or my attacker grabbing me when I tried running away. But the part that traumatized me the most was the experience of knocking on car window after car window in broad daylight at half past five in the afternoon and not a single person stopping to help. Some people had their windows down and could hear every word I was yelling: "Please help me! I've been carjacked. Please, please help me!" They could feel the terror in my voice vibrating against their car windows. Yet nobody stopped. Instead, people rolled up their windows. Women shoved me away with their hands, justifiably afraid they might fall victim to what had just happened to me. They fearfully demanded, "Get away from my car!" I looked over my shoulder, wondering if my perpetrators were running after me or if I was going to be shot in the back. As I banged on car windows, I had the horrifying thought: *What if one of these drivers is in it with the carjackers?* So I did the only thing I could do in that moment: I kept running.

So many people chose to do nothing. That was the most horrific part.

Then at a big intersection, a little old car veered across all four lanes of traffic, and a young woman rolled down her window and yelled, "Are you okay?" As I ran toward her jalopy, I yelled back, "No. I've just been carjacked. Please, can you help me?" She leaned over and pulled the little knob to unlock the car door and urged, "Get in, get in!" I leapt into the passenger's seat, and she sped away, taking us to safety.

Fast-forward a few years, and I finally realized how much that young girl inspired me. I was a stranger. She had no reason to help me, but she did.

If it wasn't for *that girl*, that young, courageous, nineteen-year-old girl who stopped and got me to safety, I don't know what would have happened. I don't want to imagine. I am forever grateful to her for risking her own safety to help a stranger. She inspired me to never be one of the drivers who turns a blind eye, pretending not to hear. Instead, I want to be *that girl*, the one who leans over, unlocks the door, and lends someone in need a helping hand. Most importantly, that girl taught me to have a heart that is willing to be interruptible to notice what God is calling me to be a part of. If the roles were reversed, I hope I would've done the same thing. What do you think you would have done? Would you have been one of the women who shooed me away? Or would you have pulled over and allowed me into your car? Whatever your answer is, it may change once you finish reading this chapter.

The truth is, I haven't always been "that girl." The brave kind. The others-centered kind. The curious kind. It's hard! It's inconvenient! It's so much easier fixating on my own plan, my own goals, and my own way that I can completely miss an opportunity to help right in front of me. I'm constantly focused on reaching that deadline or hitting that sales target, or even just sticking to my weekly routine or daily to-do list. To be a good friend, neighbor, godmother, or even a caring stranger is a constant work in progress for me. My driven heart and competitive spirit are always fixated on the task at hand. I fall into the trap of putting my responsibilities ahead of relationships. At times, I've wrongly believed that my progress was more important than others'. But as believers, our most important job is to love God and to love people (Matthew 22:37–39).

Just like my "that girl" moments, you don't have to start a foundation, raise a million dollars, or have a million followers to have an impact on someone else's life. It's simple. Notice the people around you. Pray that God would reveal who needs help that day. It really comes down to being intentional and being open to those opportunities to make a positive impact in someone's life. One of the human trafficking survivors I have had the honor of meeting went on to work as a nurse at the same hospital that identified her as a victim of trafficking. Today she is helping others because someone cared enough and was willing to be interrupted to notice and then actually do something to help her.

You can be "that girl" by noticing when a coworker seems down and taking the time to ask them if everything's okay. Or maybe you know a neighbor in need of help, so you decide to ditch your to-do list and stop by their house or call to encourage them. Let's hope we'd all be *that girl* if someone was in need like I was on the day of my carjacking, but we can also be *that girl* in the small, intentional acts of kindness or service. Be open and attentive. Who knows whose world God may use you to change forever.

WHAT *THAT GIRL* DOES

Putting others first doesn't always come naturally. It takes intentionality to choose each and every day to put others' needs before our own. I can't say I've always done it, and I've failed more times than you know. But when I catch myself getting caught up in my own problems, goals, and deadlines, I try to remember to stop and pray my personal mission statement: "Here I am, God, use me with what I've got, with where I'm standing, for Your glory." I've also learned to really mean it because it seems that God loves answering that type of prayer. When we ask, He can and will use us for His kingdom impact.

There are a few women whose lives were used in great ways to impact others just by being *willing*. These women allowed their plans to be messed up so that God's plans could be set in place. I'd like to tell you about two women who were bold enough to step up for others and inherently touched uncountable lives: Anne Sullivan and Queen Esther.

Anne Sullivan may not be a household name, but she sure found herself in a unique position to be *that girl*. Anne was Helen Keller's lifelong companion, mentor, and teacher.

The two originally got connected during the summer of 1886 when Helen's father wrote a letter to Michael Anagnos, the director of the Perkins School for the Blind, seeking a teacher for his daughter who had been deaf and blind since she was just nineteen months old.[1] Having experienced a form of blindness herself at only twenty years of age, Anne accepted the challenge. Under Anne's guidance, Helen learned braille, lipreading, and finger spelling to communicate, read, and write, eventually becoming the first deaf and blind person to graduate from college.[2] Helen wrote fourteen books and gave over 475 speeches throughout her life with Anne's help.[3] John A. Macy, a Harvard University instructor, fell in love with Anne, and she finally accepted his marriage proposal; however, she did not let her marriage affect her responsibility with Helen. Anne and her husband moved in and continued to live with Helen, and the two women remained inseparable.

As significant as Helen's accomplishments were, it's impossible to ignore the impact that Anne had on her life behind the scenes. Both helped revolutionize the field of education for individuals with sensory impairments. Both championed the cause of disability rights. Both are profound examples of resiliency and perseverance. But Anne Sullivan chose to act on behalf of one little girl without realizing the ripple effects of her dedicated work.

A few months before she met Helen, Anne gave a special valedictory address to her fellow classmates. She charged them with these powerful words: "Fellow-graduates: duty bids us go forth into active life. Let us go cheerfully, hopefully, and earnestly, and set ourselves to find our especial part. When we have found it, willingly and faithfully perform it."[4]

I think it is fair to say that Anne found her part, and she faithfully performed it.

Anne's lifelong dedication to education still inspires educators, advocates, and persons with sensory impairments. Her work is proof of the transformative power of education, communication, and guidance for people with disabilities. She has had a lasting impact on the field of special education, and her story remains a beacon of hope for people with sensory impairments so they can break barriers and achieve great things.

The second woman I want to tell you about is probably the original *that girl*. Ladies, give it up for Queen Esther! Esther's story may not be the fairy tale we grew up hearing, but it is one of bravery, courage, and stepping up to make the right decision, in the right moment, for the right reasons. While living in Persia under the care of her cousin Mordecai during the exile of the Jews (486–465 BC), the king basically threw a nationwide beauty contest to find his new queen. Guess who won? Esther. Not born of royal blood and not even born of Persian nationality, this young Jewish girl found favor in the eyes of the king and became royalty overnight. What may have been scary and overwhelming to a young girl like Esther would soon become a part of God's plan to save a nation.

The twist in the story comes when a Persian official named Haman tricked the king into making a terrible decree against the Jews. Basically, Haman proposed a plan of mass national genocide because he held a grudge against Esther's cousin, Mordecai (Esther 3:1–15). In hearing this decree, Mordecai sent word to Esther:

> Do not think that because you are in the king's house you alone of all the Jews will escape. For if you remain silent at this time, relief and deliverance for the Jews will arise from another place, but you and your father's family will perish. And who knows but

that you have come to your royal position for such a time as this? (4:13–14)

No pressure, right?!

Esther had a choice. Knowing her position of influence, she could approach the king without being summoned, risking the death penalty, and personally plead with him on behalf of her people, or she could ignore Mordecai's request and remain silent (vv. 10–12). I can only imagine Esther's thinking: *My safety versus the safety of others. Will my king really kill me if I enter the inner courtyard without his permission? That is the law . . . but my people . . . God, could it be that You really did put me in the palace for "such a time as this"?*

The magnitude of that decision gives me chills. There was no neutral position. Failure to decide would bring catastrophic loss. After three days of prayer and fasting, Esther sent this reply to Mordecai:

"*I will go* to the king, even though it is against the law. And if I perish, I perish" (v. 16, emphasis added).

Three words marked a momentous decision in human history: *I will go.*

One part of being *that girl* is choosing to *go*. Like I mentioned already, it's stepping up to do the right thing, at the right time, for the right reasons. Esther realized God put her in a unique position at a unique time to serve in a unique way. Esther decided to approach the king, and her decision did make a difference. Her courage and intervention with the king played a vital role in preventing the planned genocide. It eventually led to a new decree that saved and preserved her people (8:5–14). The Jewish people recognized her bravery and leadership, which led the Jewish community to foster a sense of unity and solidarity. To this day, Esther's boldness and courage inspire people facing adversity and challenges while emphasizing the importance of supporting one another.

Being *that girl* is recognizing where your feet are. God often puts us in places not just for our own benefit, but for the benefit of others. Like Esther, could it be that God placed you where you are for "such a time as this"? If you grew up in church, I know you've heard that before. But imagine if we really did approach our days with that mentality. Mervin Breneman, a Bible scholar who wrote an insightful commentary on the book of Esther, noted, "Many [people] are more concerned about their own security than about the desperate physical and spiritual needs of the world. If they understood that their decision could make a difference, many would make the commitment God is asking of them."[5]

While I'm not sure Esther knew the impact her decision would make, what really matters is that she chose to have courage and take that step of obedience in faith. My pastor always asks, "What would you do if you were guaranteed it wouldn't fail?" Let me ask you a different question: "What would you do—in response to people's needs—knowing that you *could* fail?" What I love about Anne and Esther and my *that girl* stories is that they all knew there was a cost. There was personal sacrifice on the line. For Anne, it was time and family. For Esther, it was the likelihood of losing her life. For *that girl* who rescued me, there was the risk of being carjacked herself. Each of them counted the cost and said it was worth it. There will always be a cost. Being *that girl* is choosing to go. Being *that girl* is having situational awareness. But more than that, being *that girl* intercedes for people no matter the cost.

WHAT STOPS US FROM BEING *THAT GIRL*?

If we understood and believed that our contribution could have a ripple effect of goodness that is potentially transformative to the people or community around us, should it not inspire us to act? If you knew one step of faith could impact even just one person for the better, wouldn't you take it? So what causes our lack of boldness and action? What is the thing that holds us back?

Like all the drivers who refused to stop for me, I often find myself intimidated by fear. I tend to get overwhelmed by complex situations that make me feel like my small actions won't be enough to address a large-scale problem. When I first got involved in the fight against human trafficking, the statistics were incomprehensible. The need is so large, and making a positive difference felt completely impossible. As of 2023, there are an estimated fifty million people trapped in human trafficking. If only 1 percent of victims could be rescued in the United States today, we wouldn't have enough beds to provide safe shelter for the survivors. How do we ever make a dent in a number like that? That's when I remember *that girl*—the one girl who stopped and used what she had—a small, beat-up old car on its last legs—to help another girl: me.

Sometimes, I'm afraid the steps I take will backfire and make me look like a fool. The fact is, our feelings can be fickle and unreliable. Just because we feel a certain way doesn't mean it's the truth or the right way forward.

One day we were sharing about the work we do at the Tim Tebow Foundation with a group of influential people who were interested in supporting our fight against human trafficking. After the briefing, an individual responded to me that, "Helping children is good and all, but what difference does that truly make? The perpetrators should be the focus." I was appalled. In my head I was thinking, *Then you go look all the kids on our safe campuses in the eye and tell them that helping them doesn't make a difference.* Not understanding exactly how our actions will make a difference shouldn't stop us from helping. We want justice as soon as possible, but supporting someone who is walking through their deepest, darkest days is our first priority.

Just about every introductory psychology textbook contains a case study called the *bystander effect.* Originally coined by psychologists Bibb Latane and John Darley in the 1960s, the bystander effect essentially says that the more people who are observing someone in trouble, the less likely each person is to help.

This psychological phenomenon came about after a tragic incident in Queens, New York. Twenty-eight-year-old Catherine "Kitty" Genovese was brutally attacked while walking home. The *New York Times* reported that several witnesses heard her cries for help, but no one intervened, leading to a prolonged assault resulting in her tragic death before reaching the hospital.[6]

Genovese's death inspired decades of research into the psychology behind why people don't respond when they should. Researchers have found three main psychological factors that are thought to contribute to the bystander effect:

- The feeling of having less responsibility when more bystanders are present = *Someone else will do it.*
- The fear of public judgment when helping = *What will people think of me?*
- The belief that because no one else is helping, the situation is not actually an emergency = *It's not that bad.*[7]

We see heroic videos of people responding to danger every day on social media and the news. The bystander effect doesn't happen in every crisis; it's a general observation that researchers have made through numerous social experiments. To be honest, we can all probably come up with some legitimate excuses to rationalize why we don't help, or don't pull over, or don't donate, or don't make that phone call to someone in need. Maybe you don't have time because you're already late for your flight, or perhaps you're confident that your other friend will check in on why Kristen didn't make it to the Bible study she never misses. Maybe it's raining and you don't want to get your good shoes dirty. Or maybe you'll "just pray for them" instead.

This list could go on and on. My point is that sometimes we find ourselves in a pickle of a moral dilemma and still try to justify our behavior for not rising to the occasion. I can only hope and pray that when presented with an opportunity to choose to love someone first, I'd choose to go and do just that. Have you ever found yourself victim to the bystander effect? What stops you from being *that girl*?

TAKE THE HARD STEPS

Doing the right thing is rarely easy. Oftentimes it requires you to take the hard, difficult, scary, unpopular, and inconvenient steps toward something or someone many others are walking right past. Every parent knows this firsthand. When I was growing up, my parents allowed me to have friends over but never allowed me to do sleepovers other than at two or three highly vetted friends' homes whose parents they knew like siblings, and even those were very rare occurrences. My mom had hard but age-appropriate conversations with me from a young age. The conversations weren't always comfortable to talk about, but I am so grateful and thankful that she never stayed quiet to protect my comfort. She empowered me with the knowledge to recognize danger from a young age. I sometimes sulked, gave her the silent treatment, and even slammed a door or two at her nos. Today, knowing the pervasiveness of child sexual abuse, I couldn't thank my mom enough for doing her job as being my mom and my protector so well. Could she have been oversensitive at times? Sure. Does it matter now? No. I don't even remember the friends' names whose sleepovers I missed out on.

It seems to me that doing the right thing means ignoring what the rest of the world is doing, overcoming your fear of the consequences, and making a choice to step in and do the right thing despite the risk to yourself, or risk living a life of regret. I don't know about you, but I hope to be remembered as the girl who stepped up to fight for those who couldn't fight for themselves. To all the mommies reading this chapter, the next section will be hard to read. As I'm writing this, I am not a mother yet, but I am a daughter and a big sister. As an anti–human trafficking advocate, I speak up for women and children who have been through the most horrendous acts of evil I never knew existed. This is me stepping in, having the not-so-easy conversation with you.

Warning: potentially triggering content below.

At one of my Unbreakable workshops, I hosted a panel conversation alongside a few ladies who are experts in the field of protecting women and children all over the world from the dangers we face. The women in the audience were provided with proactive and practical steps to look out for themselves and their families, especially on social media, where a large portion of online sexual exploitation of children happens. We highlighted the unsettling truth that abusers can be a part of our circle of trust (a parent, relative, teacher, coach, etc.). Education is key in knowing what to be on the lookout for, and it is one of the first steps to speaking up and seeking help when something doesn't seem right. After the workshop, several women reached out, realizing they had encountered situations of sexual abuse, especially in their inner circle, but had hesitated to act due to fear of consequences from speaking up. Learning from the stories that the panel discussed emboldened them to realize that they are not alone and can take action. We discussed topics similar to Marilyn Van Derbur's story. The fact that multiple women acted and sought help after hearing the discussion is why I want to share it with you too. My aim is to encourage action. Approximately one in four girls and one in thirteen boys face situations like Marilyn's.[8] So if you feel isolated or helpless, remember that you're not alone and change is possible.

In July 1957, Marilyn Van Derbur was crowned Miss Colorado, and a few months later, on September 7, 1957, she was crowned Miss America 1958. Growing up in Denver, the Van Derburs were considered "the perfect family." Marilyn was the youngest of her three sisters and succeeded in everything she did: got straight As, was homecoming queen, was on the ski team, sang in the choir, and graduated with honors. Her father, Francis Van Derbur, was a millionaire businessman, a very active philanthropist, and a role model in the community.[9]

No one would've suspected how Marilyn was suffering. A suffering she thought would never end. From ages five to eighteen, Marilyn was sexually abused. Even worse, her abuser was her father. Deeply traumatized by the evil she was experiencing, Marilyn disassociated and created split personalities in order to cope: a "daytime" child and a "nighttime" child. Her daytime child would go to school, play tag with her friends, turn her homework in on time, and smile her way through the day. Meanwhile, her nighttime child stayed at home in her room, terrified to come out. Her nighttime child hated and despised herself. She wanted to die each day as the sun went down and the darkness came out. In an interview years later, Marilyn recalled one particular night she'd never forget,

> My mother walked down the hallway . . . I was about eleven or twelve, and my father always came in late at night, late, meaning ten, eleven. Sometimes midnight. And he'd been in my room for maybe a half hour. And all of a sudden, I heard footsteps coming down. I could hear the first step. And then the second step, very, very, very slowly. And then the third step. And she was now about twelve feet from my door and I waited to hear another step. And it was just a dramatic moment when everything stopped for all three of us, all three of us knew exactly what each one of us was thinking and knew. It's the only time I ever felt my father afraid—he just stopped, and I thought it's going to be over. She's going to come in. And we waited for that dramatic moment.
>
> And then I heard a step up the steps and up the steps and up the steps. And I knew she would never come through that door. And I knew she would never, ever come to help me.
>
> I had a reporter say to me, "Did your mother know?" I said, it went on in our home for eighteen years. Of course she knew. Maybe she just couldn't deal with it. But I do believe she made a decision. I believe she made a choice and she didn't choose me.[10]

Every time I read Marilyn's story, my heart breaks. The hopelessness she must have felt. The shame and humiliation she didn't deserve to carry. Her silent screams begged for her mom to burst through the door, scoop her up in her arms, and rescue her. As terrorizing as Marilyn's childhood was, I think of the hundreds of thousands of girls and women all over the world who find themselves in similar vulnerable situations. As Marilyn said, her mom made a decision: "She didn't choose me." Her mom, for whatever reason, wasn't willing to take the *hard steps*. I'm sure her mom had reasons she used to justify her lack of action to protect her daughter. Moms reading this, if you ever suspect such evil taking place in your home or life, there is a way out. There are amazing organizations and people in this world that can and want to help protect both you and your children. If you've personally experienced this, or perhaps you suspect such behavior in someone else's life, I urge you never to stay quiet for the sake of the perpetrator's comfort. Local churches often have counselors, so call! Find your nearest police station, and call! Look up a local women's shelter; they could help point you in the right direction. If you're in school, tell a trusted teacher or guidance counselor and ask them to help you. If you tell somebody and they don't believe you, tell somebody else, but don't stop until everyone involved is safe! You matter. You are so valuable, and you do not have to endure such evil. For information on organizations that want to help you navigate difficult situations, please visit my website www.demitebow.com to access resources and find your best next step.

At the time of writing this, Marilyn is now eighty-six years old. As I mentioned in the last chapter, God can take our pain and use it for His purpose. Over the last several decades, Marilyn has been on the front lines, fighting for those who've experienced sexual abuse. She's inspired thousands all over the world, reminding them that healing *is* possible!

I'm so grateful Marilyn was willing to take the hard steps to share her story as an incest survivor. I'm also grateful for people like Queen Esther, Anne Sullivan, and *that girl* during my carjacking incident who were willing to take the hard steps to do the right thing.

Our ultimate example, of course, is Jesus. He willingly embarked on the most challenging journey in the history of the world for the sake of humanity. He walked the agonizing road to Golgotha fully aware of the excruciating physical and emotional torment that awaited Him. Being fully God and fully human, He could've stopped and called down a legion of angels to protect Him. He didn't. He knew the weight of the world's sin was heavy. He knew Roman crucifixion was torture. He knew the abandonment He would endure from His Father. Yet He pressed on. He went to the cross anyway. Not because it was a mere duty but because of an overwhelming love for you and me. Because we were worth it to Him.

Jesus chose our best interests above all else. He took the hardest steps anyone could ever imagine, offering us redemption and eternal life. In that extraordinary act, Jesus exemplified the epitome of selflessness. As believers, one of our challenges is to die to ourselves and strive to be more like Jesus so the world can experience God's love through us. It's no secret that each one of us is greatly flawed. Thankfully, we have God's Holy Spirit in us to sanctify us, helping us to become more like Jesus. Second Corinthians 3:18 says, "So all of us who have had that veil removed can see and reflect the glory of the Lord" (NLT). Striving to being more like Jesus means loving God and loving people through humility, kindness, patience, and graciousness. I will never be able to list all of Jesus' characteristics, but if I had to take my best guess on what Jesus would choose above all else, I would say that He would choose to love first. And I don't mean *love* as in the modern version of love—to have warm, fuzzy feelings—I mean *love in action*, which is to do what needs to be done to help someone else, even at a personal expense.

If you grew up in and around church, you're probably familiar with the acronym WWJD. It appears on T-shirts, bracelets, bumper stickers, tattoos—you name it! It simply stands for What Would Jesus Do? It's a popular phrase that encourages individuals to consider how Jesus might respond or act in each situation. But have you ever actually sat back and thought about the answer to WWJD? Well, a group of teenagers did. In an attempt to answer that famous question for their nonbelieving friends, they created the He Would Love First (HWLF) movement. What would Jesus do? He would love first.[11] I love it! It's the simple truth of the gospel.

Are you willing to step up, despite the inconvenience,
risking the possibility of failure
to do the right thing, at the right time, for the right
reasons,
even when that means doing the hard thing or having
the hard conversation?
Would you be *that girl* today
who chooses to love first?

EIGHT

LONGING FOR BELONGING

It was a Saturday morning on the campus of a large Southeastern Conference (SEC) college. I was killing time while Tim was doing his thing for SEC Nation on TV. As I was sitting in the cafeteria, enjoying the buzz a college campus exudes on game-day Saturday, watching the students excitedly come and go, one thing really hit me: they all looked the same. Every single girl who approached the counter to grab a drink was dressed the same from head to toe. A similar outfit, in similar brands, wearing similar shoes, and sporting their perfectly sporty fanny packs. I could even sense what the "in" drink was to buy. It got me thinking that I was in the wrong business and needed to create a specific athletic wear brand for college campuses. I'm kidding . . . maybe.

In all seriousness, why is the desire to fit in something our souls so desperately need? Today, with so much of our lives on social media where we get a front-row seat to millions of highlight reels, the "fitting in" problem has been exacerbated that much more. I mean, there are influencers out there whose only niche is to help you find that designer product "dupe," so if you can't afford the real product, you can buy a look-alike in order to fit in and look like everyone else. Ironic, right? I'm not judging here. I've done it too! Enjoying fashion and following the trends is fun. It's our motivation behind the behavior that really gets to the core of the potential problem.

I'll never forget a certain moment in college when I desperately wanted to fit in—into a parking spot! I was running late to class because I couldn't find parking. I tried my best to get into that parallel parking spot, but after a nineteen-point turn, I accepted that it wasn't going to work. There just wasn't enough room for my tiny compact hatchback to squeeze in next to the massive truck that I assume must have been driven by a guy who was overcompensating for some kind of insecurity. Breaking out into a stress sweat, I still believed that if I tried hard enough, my car would morph into a four-by-four that could get up onto the curb. I nearly lost two rims in the process; no college student can afford that (speaking from experience). I would never park in a handicap spot, so I eventually settled for parking on the yellow line (not a proud moment) and just accepted that I would get a parking ticket. I figured it would be cheaper than buying two new tires.

Have you ever tried making something work so hard, but it just wasn't happening? Trying to fit into that parking spot felt equally as uncomfortable as trying to fit into a pageant dress that was so cinched in the waist it was difficult to breathe. It is so hard to think clearly while wearing shoes that could double as stilts. But my pageant coach had made a great case: "Demi, we don't need you to fade away in a top-ten lineup, so let's fasten those straps and get walking."

Since I proudly stand at five foot six, probably a good four inches shorter than the average contestant, he wanted to give me the best chance to stand out (literally) from the other women in the lineup. I thought it was a genius strategy. So much so that I was willing to sacrifice my blistering feet. To prevent making a fool of myself, my coach and I had "ramp training" days. Yup, days where I practiced walking heel toe, heel toe, on a ramp. It still boggles my mind that ramps are one of the slipperiest surfaces ever, designed for women to walk on wearing platform heels. But I got real savvy. I carried extra-firm hairspray—the cheap and sticky kind—in my pageant bag that stayed in my dressing station backstage. I would spray it under my shoes right before show time. Rookie warning: make sure the hairspray dries before going on stage. Sandpaper or grippy tape is another option. Worst-case scenario, you can scrape your new shoes on pavement or a tar road to get rid of the slipperiness.

There were many pageant tricks of the trade. I learned all the unspoken pageant protocols just like any college girl knows the unspoken dress code on campus. Have you ever heard of a pin curl? It's an old Hollywood style of curling one's hair by using a curling wand and hair pins, preferably the steel kind. The secret is getting the curls pinned to your head while they are flaming hot and letting them cool for a good hour because that makes the curls hold longer. Or how about spraying hairspray on your bum cheeks to keep your bathing suit in place? And don't even get me started on "chicken" cutlets!

A backstage director once asked our group of models to bring chicken cutlets for the fashion show. One of the models showed up the next day with a small cooler of raw chicken breasts. I'm literally laughing out loud because I have nearly made the same mistake before; thankfully, Google saved me from actually showing up with chicken breasts and instead taught me that cutlets are fillers for your bra cup (a small-boobie girl problem), also known as "sticky boobs."

They are made of silicone, which has a raw-chicken texture, and helps fill your dress cups. That was another staple in my pageant bag and came in very handy to help prevent wardrobe mishaps.

I also always had double-sided tape and a dozen safety pins in all my bags. I learned some of these terms and tricks along the way, mostly from trial and error, but some I learned proactively. I hired professional makeup artists to teach me how to do my makeup and how to optimize my makeup products. They helped me find the right shades and colors to go with my skin tone, taught me how to apply a winged liner (by the way, sticky tape is a huge help to get that liner extra sharp!), and they enlightened me that the term "baking" is not just relevant to cupcakes.

WRINKLES ARE ROAD MAPS

In a world where women are pressured by media on all sides to conform to a certain standard of beauty, you may be wondering what the pressure felt like on a national and global stage to achieve so-called ideal standards of beauty. The truth is that as much as the pageant world has taught me about beauty hacks, I've always believed true beauty can't be forced into a box. Not by the media, not by a pageant, and certainly not by the opinions of others. Let me explain.

My childhood played a huge role in shaping my story and, ultimately, my lens for beauty. My hometown of Sedgefield was really small, surrounded by miles of forests, farms, mountains, and powdery white sand beaches with big waves knocking on the shore. Sedgefield was chosen as Africa's first official Slow Town, meaning it prioritizes a relaxed pace of life, preserving local culture and promoting sustainable practices. The area I grew up in is nicknamed "The Garden Route." Yes, everything you're imaging right now is what it looks like. If you're imagining a beautifully luscious landscape stretching miles and miles over mountains decorated by farms sprinkled across the hills and in between the valleys, creeping all the way up to the ocean shore like an overgrown ivy plant, you'd be right. I would wake up to the sweet smell of jasmine and occasionally the call of baboons far off in the distance on an early morning.

If I had to describe Sedgefield in one word, it would be *raw*. I grew up with a very simple approach to life and health in our small town with its limited options. Most of my friends' parents were farmers in the area. So we usually shopped from local farm stalls or our farmers market on Saturdays. My friends and I made hair masks from raw eggs, avocados, and coconut oil. We got our pedicures from walking on the beach and letting the sand exfoliate and the salt water heal. We weren't opposed to getting a pedicure at a spa or buying prepackaged groceries. But if the downside of small-town life was getting sent away to boarding school, the upside was a community that allowed for a slower pace, access to homegrown foods, natural remedies, and a raw and ravishing natural environment.

This had a significant impact on how we were formed to perceive beauty. We preferred a less-is-more approach. And while I know my small town with its unique setting was a far cry from many other upbringings in my home country, it's been my experience that most South African women share this preference for raw beauty. Growing up, Hollywood's glamorized beauty standards and the reality TV shows that flaunted famous families and their reconstructive plastic surgeries were closer to fiction than our reality of valuing authenticity over artificial enhancements. I'll never forget how my stepmom, Elzabé, questioned society's fixation on erasing wrinkles. She wrote a letter to a magazine eloquently expressing her views on artificial beauty enhancements.

Her words have stuck with me,

> Despite everything one can drink, apply, rub in, endure, or acquire at great cost, we will get wrinkles. The last one of us. I wonder what is actually wrong with wrinkles if it is such a common and natural process? And suddenly I realize, this is the road map of your life reflected on your face for all to read. The irritation between your eyes, the resentment of life on your forehead, the bitterness around the corners of your mouth, the superiority along your nose. Right then I decided, if I have to get wrinkles, I'm going to make sure they're in the right places. Enough laugh lines around my eyes, surprise on my forehead, and peace around the corners of my mouth. Who can argue with such a road map?[1]

I was sixteen when Elzabé wrote that letter. It wasn't just my parents who instilled a normalcy in me around natural beauty, but our public school and teachers echoed those voices. Our school rules included a no-makeup and no-nail-polish policy. We wore school uniforms, which automatically removed the pressure of having to try to fit in or avoiding getting labeled by your personal style or inability to afford the cool shoes. I believe it's an accumulation of these kinds of "simple is special" seeds that were sprinkled throughout my life that would ultimately help me navigate the world of glamour without compromising my belief in the elegance of raw, unaltered beauty. It allowed me to delight in the fun things that I loved, like dressing up and playing with makeup, without succumbing to the crushing pressure of Western beauty ideals.

HOLY SPIRIT SECURITY

I loved the beauty of the sisterhood within the industry. I witnessed girls coming to each other's aid in the middle of wardrobe malfunctions, lending shoes to someone who forgot theirs, helping fix each other's hair, and assisting with those tedious false eyelash corners that just won't stick right. I was surrounded by so many sweet women who were so secure in who they were that another girl's success was genuinely celebrated. I remember standing backstage just before the Miss Universe live show was about to start, and the girls were all hugging one another and wishing one another well. One of my fellow contestants grabbed my hand and whispered, "If I don't win, I hope you do." I mean, what a crazy sweet thing for a competitor to say! Those moments filled a longing in me to do all the sisterly things that I had always hoped to do with Franje.

But we also know there's a reason movies are made about "mean girls." None of us are immune from those experiences either. There were also women who stood up from breakfast tables when I tried to join them, made backhanded comments about me, whispered to each other, deliberately didn't clap for me, and laughed when I messed up. This type of hurtful meanness puts a lump in your throat and makes you fight back tears just so they won't mistake your hurting heart for weakness.

That kind of pettiness made me feel like I was back in boarding school. And just when I thought I'd heard and seen it all, one specific incident still managed to shock me. Shortly before the Miss South Africa finals, all twelve of us contestants were in a minivan on our way to final fittings with designers when notifications started pinging on everyone's phones. Then heads all swiveled in my direction, along with eyes and whispers and giggles. Everyone clearly knew something I didn't. Ugh! My heart still hurts for twenty-one-year-old Demi. Even though I was surrounded by eleven other women, I felt so isolated. Feeling like you don't belong is soul-crushing. Dr. Matthew Lieberman, a professor and neuroscientist at UCLA, explained the reason for the hurt I felt in that moment. He suggested our need to connect with other people is more fundamental than our need for food or shelter! In his book *Social*, he showed how our brains react to *social* pain and pleasure in the same way as it does to *physical* pain and pleasure.[2] Therefore "fitting in" is a behavioral response to what's happening in the brain.

I was shocked when I discovered that a group of contestants had emailed the Miss South Africa organization—plus the sponsors, the broadcasting channel, and the production company—to try and have me disqualified. They based this on the "evidence" that I had a coach. A coach, mind you, with no ties to the organization other than his successful track record of training former Miss South Africa winners. Basically, if a pageant was a track race, I hired the coach who trained Olympic athletes. And yup, if you're imagining the *Miss Congeniality* movie right now, you wouldn't be too far off. My pageant coach only trained one or two contestants per year, who, in his professional opinion, stood a good chance to win. What was so bizarre was that most of contestants who were calling for my disqualification had their own coaches and trainers. Some were even mentored by former Miss South Africas.

That afternoon an emergency meeting was called. I'll spare you the details but just know it was an awful moment. It's brutal to witness women tearing down other women they consider a threat. As contestants, we had spent weeks upon weeks together as roommates and shared more meals together than I shared with my family that year. We felt the same pressures and level of physical and emotional exhaustion from competing and trying to impress the judges. All of that should have led us to have compassion for each other because we were some of only a few women who have lived the same experience. Instead, tensions were stretched to a snapping point all through to the final night. It felt like the more public support I got, the more my fellow female contestants resented me. I felt more pressure from them than I felt from social media and the judges combined. Deep down, we all have a desire to be liked and to belong. I definitely had a desire to fit in with my fellow contestants. However, my job was to stand out. And I did, like a sore thumb nobody wanted to touch.

It saddens me because as individuals we were all successful, strong, and powerful, but as a group we could have done so much good for our country together. I share this story not to dwell on the past but to showcase the reality that women have the potential to be both incredible allies and, unfortunately, each other's toughest adversaries. Months after winning Miss Universe, one of the girls from the Miss South Africa competition who had initiated the recall of my participation reached out and invited me to coffee. I was hesitant to meet with her. But once again, I was surprised. I hope to never forget her words. She said, "Demi, I am so proud of you, and I am so disappointed that I focused only on my plan for my life. I didn't see God's plan for my life, and I also didn't respect His plan for your life. I am so sorry. Please, will you forgive me?" The conflict we'd faced revealed an unexpected opportunity for reconciliation and growth.

Today, I can genuinely say that I call her a friend. Her revelation taught me that when we fully believe in God's love not just for us but for all of His image-bearers, we will have a security only the Holy Spirit can embed in us.

COMPARISON KEEPS US FROM BELONGING

When I posted a poll on my Instagram and asked, "What keeps you from being your most confident self?" the common thread through the thousands of responses was, you guessed it, *comparison.* It ranged all the way from comparison of looks to the expectations of what a successful career should look like.

Comparison is a universal problem far bigger than beauty pageants that we all struggle with at one time or another. It's so easy to see other people's strengths and automatically focus on our own inadequacies. When we're comparing ourselves to others, we automatically become self-focused in that relationship. We're not focused on getting to know that person or connecting on a deeper level because comparison takes over, causing us to be insecure. When we become focused on ourselves and how we don't add up, we can't listen to someone else, get to know someone else, or champion someone else's wins or strengths.

Comparison isn't a new concept. We see it occur all throughout Scripture. Cain compared himself to Abel (Genesis 4). Leah most likely compared her beauty to her sister, Rachel (Genesis 29). King Saul became envious of David's popularity (1 Samuel 18). The older son compared himself to his prodigal brother (Luke 15). And the disciples argued among themselves about who was the greatest (Mark 9). From an academic standpoint, social comparison research dates to Leon Festinger's work in the 1950s. Leon was one of the first to identify our need to evaluate ourselves against others to determine whether we think we are *good enough* or *correct*.[3]

One of the most gut-wrenching and reassuring examples of fighting comparison is found on the shore of the Sea of Galilee. In John 21, after Jesus had already made a few appearances to His disciples post-resurrection, He decided to make another surprise visit. Peter and some of the boys had decided to go fishing. *Sounds about right.* After not catching anything all night and likely feeling depleted, Jesus appeared on shore shouting a suggestion: "Throw your net on the right side of the boat and you will find some" (John 21:6).

I can only imagine the attitudes coming from inside the boat. Throw it on the other side of the boat? We've only been fishing our whole lives. Why would the net on the other side be any different? Nevertheless, the boys obeyed (despite their disbelief) and ended up catching 153 fish in one haul! When they came ashore, Jesus was in the process of making them breakfast (vv. 10–14). Now, here comes the part I don't want you to miss. After having a very restorative conversation with Peter, Jesus proceeded to tell him how he would eventually die—apparently by crucifixion (vv. 15–19).

When Peter heard this, he turned around, saw his disciple-friend John, and responded, "Lord, what about him?" essentially asking if John would die by crucifixion too (v. 21).

Jesus simply replied, "If I want him to remain until I come, what is that to you? You follow Me!" (v. 22 NASB).

Did you catch it? In a very intimate conversation where Jesus was reinstating Peter's leadership and giving him insight into his future, Peter's first thought was *comparison*! *What about John?* It's human nature. I can relate. Jesus basically responded with, "That's none of your business, Peter." His words in John 21:22 should serve as an anthem in our life: "What is that to you? You follow Me!" (NASB).

Far too often I fall into the same comparison trap as Peter, forgetting the unique plan and purpose God has for my life. The truth that I think is being conveyed here is that Jesus doesn't want or ask us to be like anyone else. All He desires is for us to *follow* Him. He quite literally wants us to take our eyes off of other people and place our eyes on Him. Identify at least two areas in your life where you can take your eyes off others and fix them on Jesus. Here are two areas in my life:

What is it to you that she multitasks better under pressure than you? You follow Me.

What is it to you that she got invited to that event you've always wanted to go to? You follow Me.

Your turn:

What is it to you that ____________________? You follow Me.

FITTING IN IS FEAR, BELONGING IS LOVE

We have a longing deep in our souls to belong, to be accepted, to be a part of something bigger than ourselves. Peter and John understood that as they stood on the beach with Jesus. You and I are no different in our longing for belonging, for calling, for significance. We're so hungry for it that we stuff ourselves with anything to try to fill that hole. But having the perfect purse, saying the perfect thing, attending the popular event, or being part of the "in" group will never give us lasting belonging because all those things will shift or go out of fashion and eventually become irrelevant.

The only place we can truly find our perfect fit is walking in our God-given identity, belonging, and purpose—wrinkles and all. The fitting in is just a Band-Aid to a much deeper longing God placed in all of us from the very beginning: *belonging*. American pastor and theologian Timothy Keller said it so perfectly:

> To be loved but not known is comforting but superficial. To be known and not loved is our greatest fear. But to be fully known and truly loved is, well, a lot like being loved by God. It is what we need more than anything. It liberates us from pretense, humbles us out of our self-righteousness, and fortifies us for any difficulty life can throw at us.[4]

The problem with wanting to fit in is that we become *fixated* on fitting into something false, something temporary. In Genesis 2, God made it clear that being alone is not ideal. We are meant to build relationships with each other and Him. Even within the nature of God, there is a beautiful sense of community showcased by the Trinity. Belonging is what God intended for each of us because belonging is a picture of His love for us.

The blazing red flag about "fitting in" is that it is rooted in fear. Belonging is different. It is about love. *Fear* and *fitting in* share characteristics around division, doubt, insecurity, rejection, comparison, and anxiety. When we're striving to fit in with this crowd or that crowd, we're acting out of fear that we won't fit in, the fear that they'll see that we're different—or worse, flawed. We're also acting out of the fear that whispers, *If they really knew me, I wouldn't be enough*, or worse, *I'm not lovable.* Much like Tim Keller's quote, "to be loved but not known is comforting but superficial." We work and strive and bend and break to fit into the mold of who we think other people want us to be. We do this so much that by the time we finally do fit in, we're not ourselves. We may feel like we belong, but it's superficial. You know yourself all too well, and you know *they* don't know the real you; therefore, you must keep up appearances at all costs or your superficial belonging will disappear. What an awful (not to mention anxiety-inducing) way to live!

On the other hand, feeling like you belong is a much deeper connection. It's about being in a place where you can be your true self, where you're valued by others for who you are, quirks and all! You can live in peace knowing you're appreciated and loved for who you truly are. Fear of judgment or rejection has no place in a space of belonging. Belonging means embracing who God created you to be and surrounding yourself with people who do the same. A true sense of belonging should leave you humbly confident with no room for judgment or comparison and give you the freedom to genuinely love and serve others.

The difference between fitting in and belonging makes me think of playing dress-up as a kid. I'd put on my mom's dresses, her clip-on earrings, and her high heels. I felt like such a big girl, but the reality was that I was only a little girl wearing her clothes. I wasn't the intelligent, elegant adult I thought everyone else was seeing. I couldn't walk properly in those big shoes. My dress was always slipping off, and I looked like an imposter. Even though I wanted to feel important with my mom's clothes on, I just looked silly. Wearing them eventually got old because I couldn't do all the things I loved, like running, getting dirty outside, and playing games with my friends. Molding ourselves to fit in with a certain group does just that; it leaves us feeling uncomfortable and awkward. We feel that if we could just shake off the unnatural fit and be ourselves again, *then* we'd be at our best.

Now, imagine your favorite outfit: that power suit, the little black dress that fits just right and never goes out of style, the miracle jeans, or those soft sweats that feel like home and the truest version of yourself. Think of how you feel in the clothes that fit just right That is what belonging feels like.

IN HIS HANDS

Recently, an Oxford professor shed new light on one of apostle Paul's most-used phrases, "in Christ," which he used approximately 160 times! When studying the grammar of this phrase in other ancient Greek texts, Professor Teresa Morgan argued that a better translation for "in Christ" is "in *the hands of* Christ."[5] What a picture this paints!

- Therefore if anyone is *in* [the hands of] *Christ*, he is a new creature; the old things passed away; behold, new things have come (2 Corinthians 5:17 NASB1995, emphasis added).

- For the wages of sin is death, but the free gift of God is eternal life *in* [the hands of] *Christ* Jesus our Lord (Romans 6:23 ESV, emphasis added).

Think about it. To be "in Christ" is to put our life *in His hands.* It means to be dependent on Him and to trust His care. To be under His authority and power. To be protected. To be valued and loved. To *belong.* Literally, by His nail-pierced hands we are saved. It was up to Him on the cross. He was responsible for our salvation. And *in His hands* we are transformed!

The Bible says in the hands of Christ there is salvation. In the hands of Christ we are a new creation. In the hands of Christ we have a forever family. In the hands of Christ we have His authority and power. In the hands of Christ there is no shame. In the hands of Christ there is freedom. In the hands of Christ we'll never be alone. In the hands of Christ we'll be shaped to become more like Him. In the hands of Christ we can never be separated from His love. In the hands of Christ we have the hope with assurance of heaven one day![6]

Where do we belong? *In the hands of Christ.* What does that look like?

1. We are part of a bigger purpose and plan.

We were made for connection as part of the body of Christ. That means we all have a unique role to play. When I met Tim's family for the first time at their Thanksgiving get-together, it was overwhelming to say the least. I have a small family, so it was always just me and my parents until my sister joined us when I was eleven. Having gained four siblings, with significant others and multiple nieces and nephews, was a very new experience for me. I tried making myself helpful in the kitchen, but Christy, Tim's oldest sister, was already the identified master chef. I thought I'd help with capturing memories, but Katie was already on it as the elected historian of the family. I tried watching the young ones, but Casey and Peter had it covered. I tried entertaining the middle kids, but Joey was already prepared. I tried being the fun aunt, but Tim and his older brother, Robby, already exceeded at being the fun uncles. Katie noticed I seemed a little out of place, and she looked at me and said, "Don't worry, we each have our roles in the family. You'll find yours too." Sooner rather than later, my role became something between the dishwasher and the makeup artist in the family. And I love it. I love cleaning; it gives me so much satisfaction (and it also gives this introverted extrovert a little space to escape to). With a bunch of big sisters and nieces who are all into makeup, it's a pretty fun role to have.

Comparison not only kills connection, but it can also hinder the work God has planned for you to do. Just like with my role in Tim's family get-togethers, following God's role and purpose for my life gives me a bigger sense of belonging and fulfillment.

2. Belonging comes with responsibility.

When you walk in your place of belonging, it gives you a humble confidence that allows you to leave behind the striving and pretending, the judgment and comparison, freeing you to love and serve others. Walking in belonging also comes with responsibility.

My childhood best friend and I used to run track and cross-country together. She is a great natural athlete and used to make the podium in all her races. One day during peak season, a random boy in school walked past her and said, "Hello, bull legs." I don't know if this boy was trying to be mean, but that three-word phrase caused my friend so much harm. She ended up quitting track and developed an eating disorder, which led to dramatic weight loss.

Her health was drastically affected to the point where she stopped getting her menstrual cycle. It was heartbreaking seeing my once-strong, healthy, and radiant friend disappearing into a little bundle of pale skin and bones. Thankfully, with the help of her loving parents, supportive friends, and some wonderful doctors, my sweet friend slowly but surely made her way back to herself. Today, she is a dynamic wife, mom, and business owner.

As believers, we're called to be the light. We're not perfect by any means, but we can and should choose to lift others up and empower them to be who God created them to be. You have a responsibility to choose your words wisely, to never place the kind of judgment, comparison, or criticism on another person the way that boy did, whether intentional or not. We can choose to never make someone feel shame, doubt, or that they don't belong. Furthermore, we can choose to speak life into those who are struggling to find their own place of belonging.

Remember: fitting in is the opposite of belonging. Though fitting in may feel comfortable in the short-term, it will never fulfill you the way God intended. If you don't have people in your circle who know the real you, flaws and all, and love you anyway, then please stop settling for scraps. Start praying now that God would provide you with friends, connection, and community where you can truly be yourself, be loved, and belong. If you trust that your heavenly Father is good, that He never changes, and that He wants good things for you, then trust me when I say that He's got something so much better for you than the fake you and fake circle of friends you've surrounded yourself with. Sometimes, in order to receive the amazing things God has in store for your life, you have to first let go of what you thought you wanted.

It reminds me of a popular parable about a father and his daughter. There once was a father who deeply loved his daughter. He gave his little girl a strand of fake pearls that quickly became her most prized possession. The little girl loved the pearls so much because her father gave them to her. She wore them every single day and never took them off. One day the father asked his daughter, "Do you love me?" "Yes, of course I love you, Daddy!" Then he went on to say, "Do you trust me?" "Yes, of course I trust you, Daddy!" He then asked her one more question: "Would you give me your strand of pearls?" Confused, the little girl shrieked, "No!" as she grasped at her favorite necklace. She ran to her room in tears, not understanding why her father, who loved her so much, would ask such a thing of her. He *knew* how much she loved them.

Later that night, after a lot of reflection, the little girl decided that she *did* indeed trust her father. Reluctantly, she went to him and handed him her most cherished gift. He kneeled down with a smile and tears in his eyes and said, "Thank you." He turned and pulled something out of his drawer—a small blue box—and handed it to his daughter. "Open it," he said. Squealing with excitement, she opened the box. To her surprise, there sat an even *more* beautiful set of pearls. Her father went on to explain that since she was older, he knew she could be responsible with this valuable gift now. These weren't just any pearls; they were the rarest and most valuable pearls in the world. The girl, with delight in her eyes, smiled. She understood now.

This is how God must see us sometimes as His children. Sometimes we grasp at and hold on so tightly to things we think we want or need. But in reality, God just wants us to let go and trust Him. He has something so much better for us than a fake set of pearls. He has a community of belonging for you, a place where you feel loved, valued, and accepted just as He's created you to be.

He has a place for you where fear isn't a part of the equation. And He has a great plan for you that, alongside your friends and family, you can live out together. He's calling you by name, asking you to follow Him into that story.

GROW

IN YOUR OWN LIFE

Welcome back to *Your Turn* in this book. Part 3 is all about excavating purpose out of pain, partnering with God to process hard things, and finding innate belonging in our Father and heaven and with community.

CHECKLIST

My hope in Part 3 of this book is for you to:

- Understand that God can use our trials in life for His triumph.
- Address any untouched trauma and begin taking steps toward healing.
- Realize the power of your story and your voice.
- Be challenged to seek out and act obediently on opportunities to love and serve others well.
- Find freedom in eliminating comparison and understand the importance of building a strong community.

RECAP

In chapter 6, I shared the traumatic experience of being carjacked, how I processed the anxiety and fears that haunted me afterward, and how I shifted this post-traumatic burden into a tool to empower other women. Chapter 7 included the story of the woman who helped me to safety right after I was carjacked to illustrate the kind of *that girl* we ought to be. I also outlined the obstacles that keep us from thinking of others before ourselves and being the girl God created us to be. Chapter 8 explored into our innate need to belong through my experience as Miss Universe. I also dove into the difference between fitting in (fear-based) and belonging (love-based).

THE BIG PICTURE

Being held at gunpoint was an experience that truly changed me. But while it was scary and awful, it ultimately made me stronger. The carjacking also empowered me to use that experience to encourage other women to fight for their lives in vulnerable situations.

Here's the ironic part: when I created the Unbreakable campaign, my objective was to educate and equip women, with the help of field experts, on the self-defense techniques that I knew before I was carjacked to save them from being harmed. And while that mission was accomplished, something more significant happened. Working with women all over South Africa and hearing their stories actually helped me to heal from that terrible experience.

Trauma typically induces a cycle of fear, shame, and isolation. For example, we are afraid that bad thing will happen to us again; we imagine what happened was our fault; and instead of seeking outside support, we become occupied with these overwhelming emotions. As a result, we bottle up the traumatic event and the residual effects it has on our mind, body, and soul and feel even more alone, afraid, and ashamed.

Getting help, whether physical, psychological, or emotional (or all the above), is key to overcoming a traumatic event. So is understanding God's promise in Romans 8:28 that "God causes all things to work together for good to those who love God, to those who are called according to *His* purpose" (NASB). This verse doesn't tell us that "all things" are good things. "All things" mean good things and bad things. The hope, however, can be found in God's promise to somehow use even the bad things for good. Often, this means helping and serving others who have experienced similar trauma. And to do this, we must step outside of ourselves and turn our focus outward. How can we support someone else? What can we offer through our experience? What camaraderie can be discovered when together we are willing to face and learn how to heal trauma?

We all have the choice to make a positive and lasting difference. While God will not force us to make the right choice, He will, if we let Him, equip and empower us to act and do something that will bring about good. Things like looking around right where you are and saying yes to being a helpful hand or a listening ear. Or choosing to be interruptible to share the good news of the hope of Christ.

We women can be each other's greatest allies or, unfortunately, bullies. Nothing quite stings like the feeling of being left out. Whether you feel like you never measure up, never quite fit in with the cool girls, or have a hard time finding your place in this world, here's a piece of advice that has changed my thinking. While we all have an innate desire to belong, the only place we can find our perfect fit is by walking in our God-given identity. In Him we will always belong!

READ, REFLECT, AND ANSWER

Trauma can either bring us closer to God or push us further away from Him. Think of one of the hardest circumstances you have ever been through. Did it impact you to run to or away from God? Why?

Looking back, how can you see glimpses of God's love for you during this time?

When you're going about your day, interruptions can be, well, annoying. Think of the incessant pinging on your phone, a coworker who stops by your cubicle while you're finishing a report, or a stranger in a shop that won't stop chatting with you. While focus is essential to accomplish our goals and to-do lists, we need to be flexible and open to opportunities God might be giving us to serve someone else. When we read about the life of Jesus in the Bible, we find that He got interrupted quite often. We can learn from Him. When we say yes to God, His timing will not always coincide with our timing.

Who is someone in your life who is hurting that you can reach out to this week when you're tempted to wallow in your own hurdles and heartaches?

A key to living with confidence and in purpose is to remind yourself that you belong to God. In Him you find salvation, everlasting life, unspeakable joy, and a peace that passes all understanding. It's time to meditate on and memorize another scripture so you can remind yourself that no matter what others think, say, or do, you are God's child. Read, meditate on, and memorize 1 John 4:4:

> You are from God . . . and have overcome them; because greater is He who is in you than he who is in the world. (NASB1995)

ACCEPT THE CHALLENGE

Whether at home, in the boardroom, on the platform, team, or field, we are all leaders in some capacity. In chapter 8, I introduced the story of Esther in the Bible. When she was the queen of Israel, she was given a choice to do the right thing, which was really hard, or to do nothing at all. Despite fear, tradition, and uncertainty, Esther appealed to the king in order to save the people of her nation.

When you are faced with a challenge, you might have a tendency to feel incapable, not enough, unequipped, or afraid. In today's challenge, I want to offer you a different perspective when you have the opportunity to do the hard but right thing. This can apply to any situation, from saying no to a temptation to standing up for someone else to making the right career decision.

WHEN YOU FEEL . . .	CONSIDER . . .
Inadequate	The feeling as an opportunity to grow, to learn, and to stretch out of your familiar comfort zones. Ask yourself, "How can I grow through this experience instead of sabotaging or denying the call?"
Afraid or anxious	These feelings are normal, yet instead of becoming obsessed with them, pray. "Be anxious for nothing, but in everything by prayer and supplication with thanksgiving let your requests be made known to God" (Philippians 4:6 NASB1995).
Confused	Acquire wisdom by searching Scripture for an answer as well as seeking wise counsel from a person who has been in a similar situation or has more experience than you.
All of the above	Just do it. Trusting God and being obedient may not come with feelings associated with boldness, confidence, or courage. That's okay. Remember, we can choose to do what's right, no matter what our feelings tell us.

PRAYER

(Read this prayer out loud in closing)

Lord, thank You for giving me everything I need to live well and do Your will. Use me and whatever I am going through to make an eternal impact. Give me the wisdom I need to do the right thing. I trust that You will never put me to shame. In Jesus' name, amen.

PART FOUR

FLOURISH

Proclaim the LORD*'s greatness with me;*

let us exalt his name together.

PSALM 34:3 (CSB)

To *flourish* simply means "to grow well; to blossom and thrive!"[1] I love that! It can be so easy to think once we reach a certain point in life, we've made it; therefore, our growth essentially stops. But by definition, *flourishing* means "continuous growth," and I believe we never stop growing! In these final two chapters, I introduce two powerful principles that help me keep a healthy perspective on what matters most: prioritizing excellence over perfection and pursuing things that will last!

Recently, I was in the Philippines, and while I was walking around a mall, I saw a large neon sign sitting next to a large bouquet of flowers that read, "In Full Bloom." What I find fascinating about the word *flourish* is that it's rooted in a Latin word meaning "flower."[2] How beautiful is that? *To flourish is to live like a flower in full bloom.* As I've discovered over the years, we often get distracted and complicate things. In this section, I hope to bring simplicity and clarity to your life to help you thrive. In chapters 9 and 10, my hope is that you're going to:

- Understand the benefits of being all-in and focused on a task at hand.
- Learn practical ways to stay engaged in the present moment.
- Live by the principle that perfection is overrated, a waste of time, and impossible.
- Reflect on how your current goals, dreams, and priorities align with eternal significance.
- Feel ignited to run hard after what God has called you to.

NINE

PRESENCE OVER PERFECTION

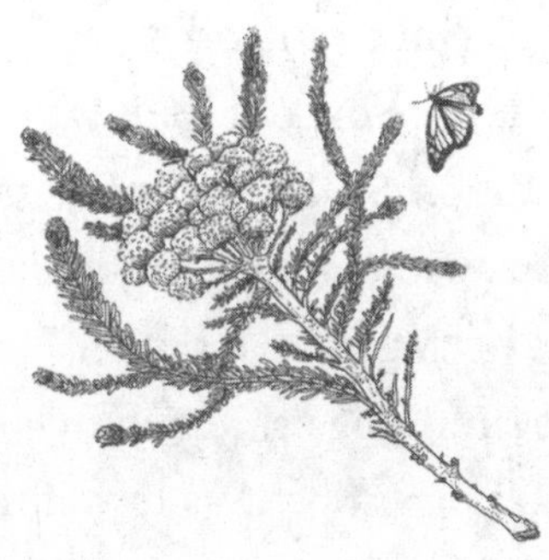

The day before our wedding a big storm hit. I'm not talking about some family drama or guests who missed their flights. I'm talking fifty-mile-per-hour winds, six-foot waves thrashing, objects flying, and a torrential downpour. That kind of storm! The weather services had predicted only one rainy day for the whole month of January, which is peak summer season in South Africa. The farming community we got married in outside of Cape Town typically relies only on winter rain. But the day before our wedding, those normal weather patterns were blown apart.

About 150 people had flown into South Africa from the US, and we genuinely had no backup for our outdoor ceremony in case of rain. I felt so much pressure. Not just as any bride who wants her wedding to be perfect, but also as an international host. Most of our non–South African guests had never been to my homeland, including all my in-laws-to-be. I felt like my wedding would reflect on my people as we made use of all the proud South African vendors. This was an opportunity for our American friends and family to get a taste of my country, my heritage, and my people. But the day before the event the circumstances were anything but perfect. We had a real problem, and time was ticking.

We South Africans have a tradition that the bride and groom do not see each other the day before the wedding, including no talking, texting, or calling. Tim and I had hosted our American-style rehearsal dinner two days before our wedding to be able to stick to this South African tradition. So the night of the storm, I was dealing with the weather drama without my partner and best friend to talk to. Talk about putting my big girl panties on!

Our options were slim! The nearest church wouldn't even hold a third of our guests. Our best bet was to wait it out and hope the weather would look better the next morning. I went to bed the night before the wedding with rain bashing against the windows and the wind howling around the corners of the building. With all the weather drama, I hadn't had time to write my vows, so I ended up staying up until midnight to get them perfect. I didn't sleep great as I was excited about our wedding day, but I was also so stressed about the weather. I tried my best to trust that our special day would still be sweet, even if everyone got soaked.

On the morning of our wedding, I got woken up at 4:30 a.m. by a rooster! I am not making this up! I tried going back to bed, but once that chicken woke me up all I could think about was what it looked like behind those curtains on the other side of the window. I could still hear the wind howling. I nervously got up and walked toward the window. *Is it thundering or are there clear skies?* Since it was summer, the sun rises early. I pulled the curtains away to reveal . . . *clear* skies! Hallelujah! Amen! Thank you, Jesus!

Because the storm had been so violent, outdoor items had gone flying, flowerpots were broken, and we basically had to rebuild the ceremony area. The circumstances weren't perfect, but it was possible to set up our venue. The wind did not die down, but the rain did not pick up either. *We'll take that, thanks!*

The rest of the day was rocky too. My bridesmaids forgot their flowers, the vintage car that drove my dad and me to the venue broke down about four hundred yards from the venue, the videographer's drone couldn't take off due to the strong winds, and I was certain the wind was going to rip my six-meter-long veil out of my perfect bun. With fists clenched under my bouquet, I stood with my dad, ready to walk down the aisle, holding on to my veil like it was a kite we were worried was going to slip out of our grasp and soar into the sky. As we stepped onto the long walkway leading to the altar, my dad looked at me and asked, "Are you ready?" I paused, took a deep breath, and realized something profound: *Nothing else matters right now. This is the moment—right here, right now.* I looked back at my dad and said, "This is it! Here we go!" The magnitude of that moment hit me in the face like a ton of bricks. I couldn't help but let loose a bunch of happy tears as we took that walk together.

We often think that moments need to be perfect to be valuable. It's so easy to get caught up in the should haves or could haves that we sometimes miss *the* moment. Your husband sending you the thoughtful text despite the chaos is *the* moment. Your mom giving you your grandma's handkerchief before the wedding is *the* moment. Your car breaking down on the way to the wedding is *the* moment. Your dad gripping your veil like it's more precious than gold to make sure it doesn't go flying in the wind is *the* moment.

Our wedding weekend is a perfect example that the moments and memories that matter are rarely perfect, but they are real and make pretty good stories to tell. Our wedding day was crazy windy, our guests were freezing, and things went flying all day, but everyone showed up with awesome attitudes to celebrate Tim and me. Our union. Our covenant. That's all that truly mattered.

A life lesson I've had to learn the hard way has been to never allow the pursuit of perfection to trump being present. There have been many moments where I look back and notice that I missed it! I missed *the* moment. It is a point in time that I will never be able to get back. If you've ever experienced a similar moment, you'll agree that it is a hard pill to swallow.

STRIVE FOR EXCELLENCE, NOT PERFECTION

There was only one perfect person to ever walk the face of this earth, and His name is Jesus. If we spent our entire lives striving for perfection, then we'd live a very defeated life because it's just not possible. Have you heard the saying, "Progress is better than perfection"? Although I agree with it, I think there is something even better than progress—excellence. At its core, *excellence* means "to excel, to rise above, to surpass, to be great."[1] I saw a cute piece of wall décor that said,

> EXCELLENCE—ALWAYS STRIVING TO DO BETTER. NOT A SKILL BUT AN ATTITUDE. THE RESULT OF RISKING MORE THAN OTHERS THINK IS SAFE, DREAMING MORE THAN OTHERS THINK IS PRACTICAL, AND EXPECTING MORE THAN OTHERS THINK IS POSSIBLE.

That's it, I thought! *That's excellence!* We should strive for better. When we aim for excellence, we focus on doing our best every day, all day. That doesn't mean we won't fail; it means we continually improve our skills, refine our abilities, and work to not repeat mistakes. Excellence is about setting a high, healthy, and attainable goal, and striving to reach our full potential.

Whenever I get invited to be a guest speaker at an event, I always put so much work into writing out my whole speech perfectly on paper. But when it comes to delivering it, I've realized it's impossible to memorize a forty-five-minute speech perfectly. I have certainly tried and failed miserably. Now, instead of trying to memorize it word for word, I work on understanding the content I am talking about through studying and learning everything I can about the subject. I explain the talk to my husband or my friends to make sure the way I am delivering it will make sense to my audience. Approaching my preparation for each talk this way gives me the freedom to get a pulse on my audience and interact with them more effectively throughout my speech instead of just dumping a ton of words on them. I get to be present, not perfect. It allows space to correct a mistake or mispronunciation in my talk with a joke or a personal comment. Best of all, it allows space for me to be human. I usually walk off the stage after delivering my speech and ask myself four questions to determine if I hit my goal of excellence:

- Did I put in the work beforehand? (Did I research and understand my topic?)
- Did I reach my goal? (Did I successfully relay the information to my audience?)
- Was I fully present? (Did I acknowledge and respond to the audience's feedback?)
- No matter how I think I did, can God use it for impact?

You can modify these four questions to help prepare and execute your task at hand with excellence too.

I believe we're called to strive for excellence in all that we do for the glory of God. Striving to do and be your best is biblical: In Daniel 6:3, we see that Daniel found favor with King Darius of Babylon because of his pursuit of excellence: "Then this Daniel became distinguished above all the other high officials and satraps, because an excellent spirit was in him. And the king planned to set him over the whole kingdom" (ESV). There are many references regarding excellence in the Bible. Here are four I always find encouraging:

- Colossians 3:17: "And whatever you do, whether in word or deed, do it all in the name of the Lord Jesus, giving thanks to God the Father through him."
- Colossians 3:23: "Whatever you do, work at it with all your heart, as working for the Lord, not for human masters."
- 1 Corinthians 10:31: "Whether, then, you eat or drink or whatever you do, do all to the glory of God." (NASB1995)
- Proverbs 16:3: "Commit to the LORD whatever you do, and he will establish your plans."

Perfection, on the other hand, often involves an unattainable goal, or at least a goal that takes longer to achieve than it should. Perfectionism is a desire for flawlessness wrapped in the fear of failure. It typically leads to unrealistic expectations and unnecessary stress. While excellence encourages growth, perfectionism can hinder progress.

PERFECTIONISM LEADS TO PROCRASTINATION

Perfectionism and procrastination are two *p*'s in a pod. (See what I did there?) *Procrastination* comes from a Latin verb meaning "to put off or delay until tomorrow."[2] Quite literally, procrastination avoids doing what needs to be done in the moment. This might surprise you, but psychologists believe procrastination is not about laziness; instead, it's a response to coping with an underlying cause such as difficulty in decision-making. It can even stem from having a lack of motivation or obsessive perfectionism. Waiting for the conditions to be "perfect" before you begin only leads to stress and anxiety over completing a project or planning that next event, so you keep putting it off again and again because it's just too much to deal with.

I regularly find myself rushing to get the most urgent item on my to-do list done, such as responding to my emails within twenty-four hours or returning a purchase in time to get a refund. Just because these items are urgent and need to be completed by a certain time doesn't necessarily make them the most important. The most important thing on my to-do list, like filing my taxes or setting up a retirement account, gets put on hold because it is more complex, takes more brain power, and needs more time to complete. Approximately 15 to 25 percent of people regularly engage in procrastination as a way of dealing with tasks that they don't want to deal with.[3] Guilt plays a key role in procrastination—dillydallying when you know you need to do something leads to feeling guilty, which leads to feeling bad about yourself, which leads to more procrastination, which leads to more guilt. You get the point. Perfectionism leading to procrastination can be debilitating.

We get so caught up in being the perfect host, planning the perfect dinner party, and making sure the house is spotless that we eventually shut down and decide having people over isn't even worth it. When you feel you must always be put together and present the perfect version of yourself, you don't leave any room for the authentic and messy side, which is glorious!

Tim and I have a sign at our front door that reads,

WELCOME, I HOPE YOU LIKE DOG HAIR.

We mean it. Our home won't always be tidy or clean. But we hope it will be warm, welcoming, and comfortable and smell like a mixture of wet dog, bacon, and a whiff of pumpkin spice. That's Tim's favorite scent, and we keep pumpkin spice candles burning year-round. The Roomba runs overtime and still makes no dent. Kobe, our golden retriever, gets in the pool just to drag his wet, floofy body over my freshly mopped floors. Chunk's slobber, or slingers rather, are all over our walls like works of art. And Paris's hair and paw prints are all over our (white) couch.

We love our home. We love our little furry family, and I always joke and say we don't have a front door; we have revolving doors instead. We always have people at our house, and our friends know exactly where to find the silverware (and the pantry). I wouldn't want it any other way. The people in our life who matter don't mind the chaos. They are all for it too. It wasn't always that way. One of Tim's and my first real married fights came after he kept telling people it was okay to come over day after day for what felt like a few consecutive weeks. I felt exhausted as I used every free minute I had to clean and cook and host and make sure everyone was having a good time. Instead of expressing my exhaustion from feeling like I had to make everything perfect, I told Tim that I didn't want to see another person for at least three months. I admit, that was dramatic, and Tim later agreed that having people over all the time was excessive. But Tim, being the baby of five siblings, was used to having people around all the time while growing up. It was a big contradiction to my experience growing up as an only child for the first part of my life, who experienced every visit from friends as a big occasion.

As we worked through our differences, Tim said, "You don't have to spoon-feed people. They are grown-ups and can take care of themselves." Lightbulb moment. *Yeah, if they don't like me without makeup, that's their problem. They can pour their own drink. And if the toilet paper runs out, surely someone can speak up and ask for more.* Tim helped me learn how to welcome people into my imperfection, and I eventually grew to accept that everyone's idea of fun didn't solely depend on my hosting. I also learned (and continue to learn) that asking for help or asking people to help themselves does not equal being a bad or imperfect host.

Being a perfectionist isn't necessarily a bad thing; it shows how detail-oriented, self-disciplined, and motivated someone can be, essentially pointing out how much they care about a goal, topic, or person. But when perfectionism leads to challenges like toxic stress, anxiety, isolation, and procrastination, it can take a toll on our mental and physical health. It slows us down and hinders productivity. Perfectionism causes us to become overly focused on the small details so that we spend excessive time on things that probably don't need that much attention.

Dr. Fuschia Sirois, a professor of psychology at Durham University who has researched the causes and consequences of procrastination for more than twenty years, talked about how procrastination is often misunderstood. She said while many believe that improving time management or self-control will solve procrastination, the truth is, that's only addressing the symptoms, not the root causes. Procrastination is primarily driven by emotions. It's not the task itself we're avoiding but the negative emotions it triggers.[4]

When feelings like anxiety, self-doubt, or frustration arise (all feelings that can be associated with perfectionism) and we choose to procrastinate, we're essentially saying, "I don't want to deal with these feelings right now." Putting off the task again and again creates more and more guilt, and the cycle continues. I mean, we've all been there. Whether it is putting the hard conversation with a colleague on hold or pushing out the first day back in the gym, we've all delayed that thing we're dreading. It's much easier to "do it later" than to deal with the hard emotions that accompany the reasoning behind the procrastination. In the end, it's hurting us much more than helping, and it's an unhealthy cycle we need to make ourselves aware of and take action to break it. Awareness is the first step to identifying those perfectionist tendencies and the moments where we want to procrastinate. We can then start putting habits into place that help us move through our procrastination and related emotions and tackle that task we've been putting off. Now that you see the negative effects of perfectionism, let's look at what the positive power of being present can do.

POWER OF BEING PRESENT

I love playing a game with my friends when we're at a restaurant, trying to see if we can spot which couples are likely to have a second date and who's probably not seeing each other again. The couples who like each other are easy to spot. Their phones remain untouched, and they engage in deep conversation with each other. Their words flow effortlessly, and the laughter is genuine as they exchange stories, dreams, and thoughts. The warmth of connection and the joy of their being fully present is nearly contagious. Unfortunately, the preoccupied, disconnected presence of a couple not making any relational progress is also contagious. They constantly check their phones, the guy misses out on half of the conversation while checking the football score, and the girl is more worried about fixing her hair than learning about his interests. I sometimes start feeling anxious just looking at the latter version in the restaurant.

While I know striving for perfection is a futile pursuit, I also strongly believe that God created us to enjoy His creation, enjoy connection with one another, and be present in the everyday moments of life. We've already talked about how our souls are hardwired for connection, and you cannot connect on a deeper level with someone if your mind is always elsewhere. I believe God created this world with so much beauty to behold, and He doesn't want us to go through life only to look up at the end and realize we missed it.

Being present means being aware of your surroundings, engaging with others around you, and truly listening to others. It means noticing the cute little storefronts, the blooming flowers, and the humor in something simple. It also means noticing the teen girl you could quickly help in the bathroom who didn't realize her skirt was tucked into her tights, the tired mom trying to wrangle a stroller through the heavy store doors, or the cashier having a bad day who needs a smile. It means we are keenly aware of the moment we're in rather than being distracted by this morning's flat tire, tomorrow's stressful presentation, or worrying about cleaning out the guest room for your in-laws. When we are intentionally present, we get to experience some of God's greatest gifts to us—His *joy* through the gift of other people.

Happiness is based on our circumstances. It's a fickle feeling that can change at any moment. One minute you're happy because your boyfriend sent you flowers and the sun is shining; the next moment you get a bad grade on a final, and bam, your happiness is gone.

Joy, on the other hand, is a fruit of the Spirit. Joy is an inner posture of the heart that trusts in our Creator and trusts in His greater plan. Joy is a heart-posture you can have no matter what the circumstances look like around you. In chapter 2, I mentioned the call (and fax!) I got from my dad and stepmom on my tenth birthday. Receiving news that I was going to be a big sister was one of the happiest moments of my life! But I tell you what, every time I had to watch Franje suffer from a seizure, happiness was the last thing on my mind. Since her passing, I do experience both happy and difficult moments, but with every thought I have, there is now a ribbon of joy that puts a smile on my face because I know God has used her life to increase my trust in Him!

Being present doesn't just mean "not distracted"; it also means using each moment as an opportunity to be a part of something bigger than ourselves. In his popular book *Don't Waste Your Life*, pastor John Piper wrote, "You get one pass at life. That's all. Only one, so don't waste it."[5] It's a blunt wake-up call to check yourself. What are you doing with your life, and why are you doing it? His book pulls on the heartstrings of all of us who get lost in the meaningless pursuits of the things that are fleeting, the things of this world, or the things that don't bring our life real value.

Wasting our lives would be living in a state of constant distraction, always looking to the next thing and missing all the beauty God has in store for us along the way. When I think back to my year after Miss Universe, I was terrified about answering the "what's next" question because I had no idea how to answer it. You would've thought I was the happiest girl in the world. Sure, I could've put on a smile, but internally I was questioning whether all my efforts were indeed meaningless. Why did winning cause more confusion about my future instead of making it clearer? The intense pressure to figure out "what's next" rained on my parade. My feelings of meaninglessness clouded my ability to really process what was an incredible year. The waiting God gave me should've been a prime time to cherish and appreciate more moments, but instead I let the uncertainty distract me.

I'm reminded of another book that has a similar thread of

caution: Ecclesiastes. Written by King Solomon, who the Bible describes as the wisest man who ever lived, this book is more like a diary by someone who has experienced a lot in life. King Solomon had everything and got to sample every earthly pleasure this world had to offer. He had all the riches he could ever want and access to all of the beautiful women in the kingdom. And yet, he still felt empty.

In our present age, we see the richest and most beautiful people in the world get divorced, and some of the biggest stars sadly end up in rehab. Their earthly possessions and pleasures could not make them happy, fulfilled, or complete. King Solomon was telling us that no matter how hard we work or how much we have, we can still be left feeling empty. Ecclesiastes may seem like a dark, contradicting, pessimistic, and confusing outlook on life, but woven throughout is a secret thread: *joy*.

The BibleProject offers this definition of joy: "Biblical joy is more than a happy feeling. It's a lasting emotion that comes from the choice to trust that God will fulfill his promises."[6] Seven times Solomon encouraged people to enjoy life![7] Ecclesiastes 3:12–13 says, "I perceived that there is nothing better for them than to be joyful and to do good as long as they live; also that everyone should eat and drink and take pleasure in all his toil—this is God's gift to man" (ESV).

If I'm being honest, it's easy for me to get caught up in my daily to-do list, that next opportunity, or fulfilling my dream of launching my own business. Putting all our focus on reaching that next goal, getting that promotion or pay raise, or getting that next degree so we can put more letters behind our name can be tempting. None of those things are bad things to pursue. I just think we can't become so distracted by the end goal that we forget to look up and enjoy where we are right now.

Remember when I told you about my rigorous training and endless preparations for Miss South Africa? What I didn't tell you was that I completely missed the moment of appreciating the previous three years that went into earning my college degree before winning that title. I was so set on winning the pageant that I refused to miss a moment. As a result, I sacrificed celebrating another milestone moment that I will never get to relive. I drove two hours to my college town, slipped on a graduation dress in the parking lot, grabbed the robe from my parents at the auditorium entrance, crossed the stage, shook the dean's hand, snapped a photo, and hit the road back to the Miss South Africa competition duties. Of course, we will need to make sacrifices for the things that are important to us, but I was not going to get disqualified from Miss South Africa for attending my graduation. I was so fixated on the future that I didn't think twice about what I was willing to exchange for something that wasn't even tangible yet.

When you beat your previous record time when training for that 5K race, God wants you to stop and look up at the beauty He's created around you to run in. When helping your child for the next test after a long day at work, God wants to make sure you enjoy the excitement your child shares with you when they get that A+. While these pursuits aren't bad, we need to stop and *enjoy* our lives too. And we can enjoy these beautiful moments in life because we trust the One who created them.

A few things I enjoy in between the imperfect moments:

- My thoughtful husband bringing me a cup of coffee after I had a bad night's sleep.
- Getting home to overly excited pups but enjoying their yips and squeaks because it signals they love me and couldn't wait to see me.
- Seeing the sunrise on the way to the airport to catch an early flight.

- Working late at night but seeing the Southern Cross constellation that only appears later in the Northern night skies.

Can you see the sweet moments in between the bitter situations? List out a few of your own.

GRATEFUL FOR GRACE

The word *gratitude* in both biblical Greek and Latin is rooted in the word *grace*. Coincidence? Absolutely not. Gratefulness is an overflow of recognizing and celebrating God's grace in our lives! Grace means getting something we do not deserve. In our lives, the absence of presence often leads to a lack of gratitude and a failure to recognize the profound grace that we've received. When we're not fully immersed in the present moment, it becomes challenging to appreciate the gifts we've been given without earning them. Gratitude, in essence, is understanding the eternal nature of these unearned blessings that His grace has bestowed upon us without condition or merit.

Think back to when you've received something you didn't deserve. One of my friends calls it her "grace pants story." She unreasonably fought with her husband one night out of anger. Instead of holding it against her the next day or giving her the cold shoulder, her husband went and bought her a cute pair of Nike shorts she'd been eyeing for a while. From that day on, she coined a phrase in their household: "putting your grace pants on." He chose not only to forgive her, even though she hadn't asked for forgiveness or even admitted her fault in the matter, but went the extra mile to get her a gift. She said that day he gave her two things she didn't deserve: the shorts and grace. What a tangible picture of grace. In other words, if we've truly been hit by the grace train and experienced the transformation from death to life, been truly forgiven of all of our past, present, and future mess-ups and failures, then we can't help but wake up with gratitude each day for what He has done. Furthermore, walking in that grace (that is new every morning, thank you, Jesus!) gives us *joy*. It makes perfect sense!

The concept of grace is what sets Christianity apart from other religions. This distinction became evident during a British conference where scholars and theologians from various corners of the world convened to explore whether there was a belief unique to Christianity. They brainstormed numerous possibilities, considering divine attributes, resurrection, and miraculous signs and wonders. However, each of these elements had parallels in other faiths. The debate persisted until the arrival of C. S. Lewis, who, in his characteristic straightforward manner, inquired about the discussion's purpose. His colleagues explained that they were seeking Christianity's unique contribution among world religions. Lewis, without hesitation, declared, "Oh, that's easy. It's grace." Upon further deliberation, the consensus was reached. The idea of God's love freely given, without conditions or prerequisites, defies the natural inclinations of humanity. Other belief systems' code of law or covenants all offer methods to *earn* divine approval. It is only in Christianity that the daring principle of unconditional love from God is embraced.[8]

Grace, in its essence, represents the divine gift offered to us because we can never attain perfection through our own efforts. The quest for perfection is a journey that inevitably eludes us, for we'll never be faultless. However, we can find contentment in the realization that we can be present, thanks to God's presence in our lives. His perfection serves as a bridge, allowing us to embrace the moment, bask in gratitude, and acknowledge the grace we've received without ever earning it.

In his book *Ruthless Trust*, modern contemplative Brennan Manning (1934–2013) shared an interesting parable about a monk being pursued by a tiger:

> The monk raced to the edge of a cliff, glanced back, and saw the growling tiger about to spring. The monk spotted a vine dangling over the edge of the cliff. He grabbed it and began shimmying down the side of the cliff. *Whew! Narrow escape.*
>
> The monk then looked down and saw a quarry of jagged rocks five hundred feet below. He looked up and saw the tiger poised atop the cliff with bared claws. Just then, two mice began to nibble at the vine. *What to do?*
>
> The monk saw a strawberry within arm's reach, growing out of the face of the cliff.
>
> He plucked it, ate it, and exclaimed, "*Yum! That's the best strawberry I've ever tasted in my entire life.*"[9]

I hope that story made you laugh, even if just a little. The moral of the story is that if you are always looking back at your past (the tiger waiting to eat you) or always looking forward to the future (the jagged rocks below), focus on the beautiful (and delicious) things in the present (like the juicy strawberry).

As I write this, sitting in my living room (probably on some dog hair), I can't help but have a big smile thinking about the last few years since my wedding day with Tim. We've certainly had our "tiger" and "jagged rock" moments, but they don't even compare to our "strawberry" moments. Amid the chaos of wedding planning and managing the storm's effects on our wedding, I remember receiving a text from my then soon-to-be husband. Correction: since we weren't allowed to communicate the day before the wedding per our South African tradition, Tim sent the text to a friend, who sent it to my friend, who then sent it to me.

He had written:

> Dear Princess,
>
> Where do I start? And what can I say? It's been 645 days since I made one of the best decisions of my life to reach out to you. It's been 638 days since my heart melted by the hope in your voice and the cuteness in your accent. It's been 631 days since I got to meet my one and only. It's been 598 days since I said these 10 magical worlds, "Does this count . . . Demi-Leigh Nel-Peters, I love you." It's great to count all these numbers and reflect just how much my life has changed as you have completely stolen my heart. But none of these numbers compare to the real number of one. My one and only, my one true love and my forever and always. Demi-Leigh Nel-Peters, I love you so much, and I cannot wait to watch you walk down that aisle and take your hand in marriage as we begin the greatest journey of our lives. Sleep well, my princess, and I will see you tomorrow.

I wrote the following for my friend to text Tim's friend, to forward to Tim:

> I love you, Timmy! I can't wait to be your wife! I hope you have the best rest tonight. Thank you for giving me so much to look forward to, not just today but every day! I go to bed tonight with a content heart, knowing fully that our best days are yet to come. See you at the altar, my sweets. We're going to crush this.

Through the storm, stress, and unplanned chaos, we took a moment to notice the strawberry, to send a text, and to be grateful for the moment. Take some time to think through what juicy strawberries you might be missing out on because you're always reminiscing on the good ole days, or too focused on the bad weather the day before your wedding. Stop and look around. Look at the smiling faces of your loved ones. Put down the phone when your child wants to tell you a funny story from the day. Take a minute to appreciate the squirrel holding a little snack in its two tiny paws, even if it aggravates your dog.

Remember, God has created you to enjoy the present.

TEN

SAY NO TO CELERY

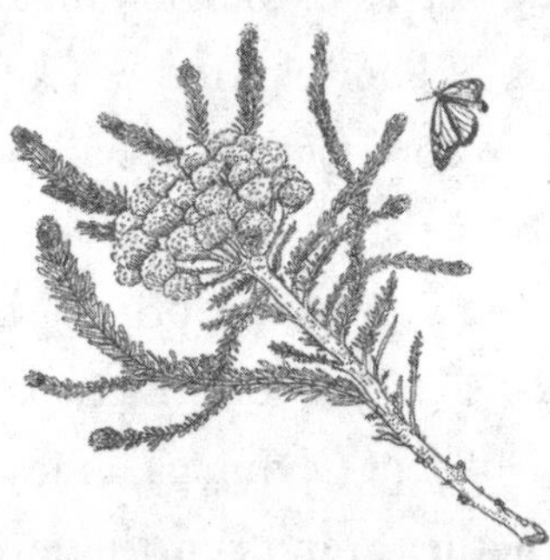

One of the most unforgettable experiences I've had was attending the Special Olympics World Games in Berlin, Germany, in 2023 with Tim. Witnessing the exceptional talent and unwavering determination of the athletes with intellectual disabilities was truly inspiring. The medal ceremonies were my favorite. The pure joy in their smiles and the tears running down their faces served as a testament to how much receiving that medal meant to so many of the athletes. It was a symbol of their dedication and a reminder that the sacrifices they had to make to overcome so many challenges and obstacles were worth it.

After the Special Olympics, Tim and I decided to make the most of our time in Europe. So we extended our stay and embarked on a journey to Athens and Corinth, Greece. We explored ancient sites and retraced the footsteps of the apostle Paul, who had spread the gospel throughout the Mediterranean. It was a trip that had a profound impact on us. We learned a lot, savored delicious cuisine, and captured countless cherished memories.

One highlight of our Corinth visit was exploring the ancient ruins. Imagine finding the ruins of a city like London or New York two thousand years from now; that's kind of what Corinth is. Corinth holds a special place in history as the city where Paul planted an early church and where two of his letters found in the New Testament were addressed to: 1 and 2 Corinthians. In its prime, Corinth was a bustling hub as its location made it a prime spot for the buying and selling of goods.[1] Kind of like an ancient version of Fifth Avenue in New York City. Paul had lived there for a year and a half, establishing Christian communities while practicing his trade as a tentmaker (Acts 18:3–4). Corinth wasn't just renowned for commerce; it was also a hub for athletic competitions. You've probably heard of the ancient Olympic Games, but you might not be as familiar with another grand sporting event that rivaled the Olympics: the Isthmian Games.[2]

The Isthmian Games were one of four major athletic contests in ancient Greece. Today, you could probably compare them to our four major tennis tournaments, including the US Open, the Australian and French Opens, and Wimbledon. The Isthmian Games took place less than ten miles from Corinth in the city of Isthmia and were held every two years in spring. These games drew thousands who came not only to witness athletic prowess but also to join in the accompanying festivities.[3] I imagine it being like what Jacksonville, our home city, is like when one of the major golf tournaments takes place here; all the restaurants are packed, hotel prices spike, and you can't ever find parking.

Corinth was obviously a hub of activity during these games. Many scholars believe that Paul and his associates attended the Isthmian Games in AD 49 and 51, utilizing the event as both a business opportunity and a platform for evangelism (Acts 18:11–12). Now you might be wondering, *Okay, Demi, thanks for the history lesson, but what's the point?* Hold on for a moment. Context is essential. In 1 Corinthians 9:24–25, Paul wrote,

> Do you not know that in a race all the runners run, but only one gets the prize? Run in such a way as to get the prize. Everyone who competes in the games goes into strict training. *They do it to get a crown that will not last*, but we do it to get a crown that will last forever. (emphasis added)

In this passage from Paul's first letter to the Corinthians, scholars believe Paul is most likely referencing the Isthmian Games. I had read this passage countless times without fully grasping its significance. But the more I delved into it, the more I discovered a principle that not only made sense of this former Miss Universe's identity crisis but, I believe, holds the key to all of us living a truly meaningful life: *having an eternal perspective.*

When Paul wrote 1 Corinthians, he knew the Christians reading it would understand his athletic references. In the Isthmian Games, there were several races that varied in distance; however, they all took place in a stadium with a dirt track approximately six hundred feet long.[4] In each race—whether short, middle, or long distance—the runner's mind was completely focused on winning. Paul knew this and drew on that local reality when he said, "Do you not know that those who run in a race all run, but only one receives the prize?" (v. 24 ESV). Everyone knew there was only *one* winner for each event. As a track runner in high school, knowing only the winners got a prize was a little dagger to the heart. The feeling of watching your opponents get the medal while you need to politely cheer was never a fun feeling. Even worse, in Paul's time the losing athletes would get severely shamed. To lose was a disgrace. First-century Stoic philosopher Epictetus wrote,

> In the [games] you cannot just be beaten and then depart, but first of all, you will be disgraced not only before the people of Athens or Sparta or Nikopolis but before the whole world. In the second place, if you withdraw without sufficient reason, you will be whipped. And this whipping comes after your training which involves thirst and broiling heat and swallowing handfuls of sand.[5]

Every athlete knew it wasn't enough to "just take part," so they put everything on the line to win—sometimes even their own lives. Competing was a serious life-or-death business. Ancient athletes, much like our athletes today, would put themselves through a ten-month monitored training period that included abstaining from wine and having a rigid diet.[6] They had their eyes, their focus, and their very lives set on the prize. I'm not sure about you, but when I first learned about this, I was so curious to find out what on earth the prize was that they would get. *Surely, it was a good one if they were willing to put their lives on the line for it.*

The reason Isthmian athletes put their mind and body through rigorous pain and discipline was to win a crown. *Okay that's pretty cool, I resonate with that.* The crown was made of withered celery or pine leaves.[7] *What? Are you joking?* I love my wellness green drinks, but celery is no prize, and it's especially not something worth putting your life on the line for. Most modern refrigerators have a special drawer that is climate controlled to keep your produce fresh longer. No matter how many tips and tricks we apply from Pinterest, one thing is evident: the fresh produce (especially the celery leaves) remains temporary and does not last.

Think about it. Athletes would spend years of their lives training to win a crown made of *celery.* Paul described this type of crown as "perishable" (1 Corinthians 9:25 ESV). *You bet!* The withered produce in my refrigerator drawer can attest to that. The prize these dedicated athletes would win was a crown that simply could not endure. You might laugh at the silliness of their efforts, but fast-forward two thousand years, and we're still striving for the same temporary things. Instead of discipline for the sake of a "head salad," it's discipline for the sake of our bank accounts, likes, views, medals, trophies, and titles. Much like the athletes competing in the Isthmian Games, we're still chasing after what those temporary crowns represent: status, admiration, respect, significance. My Miss Universe crown is made of 500 diamonds and 120 pearls. Even though it is physically somewhere safe, the significance, worth, and value that the crown was supposed to bring me did not last either.

Trophies and awards—even my Miss Universe crown—are not *bad* things; they just can't be our *everything.* As I've shared, I worked hard to win that physical crown, but it was temporary. Without question, it was a great honor and something that brought me so much pride and so much joy; it was the physical representation of all the years of hard work and grit I'd put into that competition. But that crown, along with the significance I felt while wearing it, didn't last. As soon as the new Miss Universe was announced, I handed the crown I'd worked so hard for over to the new winner, leaving me feeling vulnerable, stripped down, and without a clue as to what to do next. That's what the pursuit of temporary things does; it leaves us forever feeling like we're lacking.

The crown that Paul said believers should be trying to win is an *eternal* one. It won't rot or wither; it will last. Instead of leaving you feeling empty, this crown is one that fulfills a void deep down in our souls we didn't even know we had. This crown anchors us in our God-given identity, allowing us to walk in God-confidence that we are where we're called to be and doing what God called us to do. The pursuit of this far-superior crown requires dedication, surrender, relentless focus, rigorous training, self-denial, a mission mindset, and a genuine love for others. It's through the pursuit of the lasting crown that God allows us to make an impact for His kingdom. Now, I don't know about you, but to me *that* is a crown worth pursuing—a crown worth a lifetime of effort.

ETERNAL PERSPECTIVE

Have you ever been to a 3D movie before? If you have, you know that what you see without the special 3D glasses is much different from what you see when you put your special glasses on. Without the special glasses, the picture looks blurry and a bit confusing. I mean sure, you can get the gist of what's going on, but you're definitely not seeing it clearly. When you have your 3D glasses on, you see the movie in a whole new way. You get to see the items whizzing past your head, the characters jumping out at you, and sometimes you even feel like you're a part of the movie. It's a totally different experience from just sitting in the comfy chair and observing the action on the screen. I think that's a great example of having an eternal perspective; viewing life's circumstances through an eternal lens changes the way we look at the situation altogether. A key element to living life in view of eternity means just like Jesus, we choose to love people first.

When we view life through our special glasses with eternal lenses, we don't waiver when we are faced with the inevitable challenges of life. We can make the hard decisions and stand firmly planted in the path set before us. We can look at adversity as blips along the way to our ultimate goal: heaven.

As you reflect on Paul's athletic imagery, it's important to note that when he said "everyone who competes in the games" (v. 25), he was not saying Christians should compete against one another. Unfortunately, this happens all too often. Church against church, ministry against ministry. Believers can sometimes compete over who is theologically correct. That is definitely not what Paul meant. Elsewhere in the New Testament, Paul emphasized the importance of unity (Ephesians 4:3). There's power when we come together, not when we compete against one another. So the emphasis in 1 Corinthians 9:24–27 is not on rivalry; it's on commitment, effort, and *perspective*.

Pastor Steven Furtick of Elevation Church said in a Facebook post, "Your perspective will either become your prison or your passport. It will either confine you to the way things are or launch you into the way things are meant to be."[8] There's profound wisdom here.

Gaining perspective in life can be quite challenging, while losing it is surprisingly easy. If anyone in your household calls you "Mom," then you probably understand this concept more than most. My friends who are moms have shared with me that one minute you're staring at your kids, tears in your eyes, because of how much you love them; the next moment you've locked yourself in the bathroom for just one minute of peace. It's in those challenging moments when you gain perspective by remembering how fleeting the years are when your children are small, and it's only a short time in comparison to your whole life that your children truly need you. Perspective allows you to look at the bigger picture, which then makes a lot of those problems or challenges seem much smaller and easier to overcome.

Our English word *perspective* is rooted in the idea "to look through."[9] Perspective allows us to see beyond the surface. It's a mental lens built by beliefs and experiences that empowers us to perceive the world not merely at face value. An eternal perspective holds even greater significance. It encourages us "to look through" immediate circumstances and move forward, in light of eternity, knowing that in Christ we have purpose, hope, and ultimately victory because we know how this story ends.

When my parents first learned of my sister's diagnosis and short life expectancy, they were of course devastated and had to deal with a lot of hard moments and decisions. But instead of succumbing to fear and despair, they chose to cherish each day as an opportunity to make sweet memories with their two daughters. By seeing that trial as a temporary chapter in the grand narrative of our coexistence with God, they found resilience and a sense of purpose, understanding that their journey extends far beyond the confines of this mortal coil. Their eternal perspective empowered them to face adversity with courage and grace, even in the most trying of times.

To build an eternal perspective and to say no to crowns made of "celery" (the relentless pursuit of the temporary things of this world) and say yes to what matters most, we need to define the purpose God planted in our hearts and, like the Isthmian athletes, run after it with all we've got. Now let's explore what an eternal perspective looks like in the midst of our everyday lives.

1. An Eternal Perspective Knows That the Tallest Trees Catch the Most Wind

Facing trials in this life isn't just a possibility, it's an inevitable fact. Jesus promised that we would have many trials (John 16:33). No human who's ever lived has escaped the problem of pain. Because of the fall of man, brokenness became a part of the deal. But having an eternal perspective means we can stand firmly in the face of adversity. My hometown of Sedgefield was surrounded by mountains and forestry. Whenever I faced trials, my mom told me not to worry because "the tallest trees catch the most wind." What she meant by that is when we pursue our God-given calling, the Enemy usually has his knife out for us and will do anything to derail us from God's perfect plan. When I feel like I am catching a lot of "wind," I try to acknowledge where the adversity stems from by remembering the eternal perspective my mom shared with me. I can stand firm in the face of my hardship because I get to rely on my God-given root system that can't be shaken.

Consider the wild fig tree located in Echo Caves, Ohrigstad, South Africa. Even though it is not the tallest tree, it has the most extensive taproot ever documented. This remarkable root extends to an astonishing depth of nearly four hundred feet.[10] Can you even imagine how deep this tree's roots run? That's the depth and the length of a football field! With such incredibly deep roots, the tree is anchored firmly to the ground. Even when fierce winds and raging storms assault its branches, the tree remains steadfast. It may sway, bend, or even have a few branches ripped off, but it never breaks. This tree serves as a profound visual representation of the strength that comes from having roots firmly planted in the gospel of Jesus. You may doubt your identity after a stranger makes a backhanded comment, you may suffer the loss of someone close to you or feel stuck having to live up to the label (or Miss Universe sash) that was placed on you, but with your roots firmly planted deep within God's unchanging and unwavering promises, you become *Unbreakable*.

Having an eternal perspective when facing all of the trials of life requires an immense amount of faith. We get to have faith because of one profound truth: God always keeps His promises. Grasp on to these simple concepts: God's character never changes, and He loves us with an unconditional love. With these beliefs firmly established, we can look at the hardships of life knowing somehow God will redeem them. And in His time, we will see the good that comes from knowing our identity in Him. I learned not to bank on a crown that I only got to keep for 387 days. I saw one particularly sweet purpose that came from Franje's life after she introduced me to my husband and discovered that our waiting is often where God is most deeply at work.

2. An Eternal Perspective Remembers the Meter Stones

Over the last few years, I've had the honor of speaking at Her Song's milestone celebration. Her Song is an arm of the Tim Tebow Foundation's human-trafficking survivor care ministry in the United States. Joining them at their annual Celebration of Milestones event is a humbling opportunity where I've been able to speak with the team and the courageous women in the program. We don't call this a graduation ceremony because "graduation" often means you are done, accomplished, moving on. A milestone, however, marks a significant event in your life. Many in the program are celebrating sobriety, signaling how long they have stayed in the program. Part of the struggle is to be brave enough to stay. So even if they are not graduating, they are being celebrated for what they have done and will do!

In a more literal sense, a milestone is a stone set up beside a road to mark the distance in miles to a particular place. But as I've mentioned throughout this book, we say things a little differently in South Africa. We don't call them "milestones," we call them "meter stones"! In high school, one of my favorite sports was running track and cross-country. I remember in races, I would see little flags along the way that would mark the distance I had run so far. And man, they were such a big encouragement to me! They would remind me to keep going, to keep running. It was a visual encouragement that told me I didn't come this far to quit! In life, I believe God gives us these meter-stone moments as well. God's meter stones are those times where we've seen Him show up. They serve as a reminder of His kindness and the progress we're making!

In Deuteronomy, Moses told the second generation of Israelites to go and set up a physical milestone to remind them where God had brought them from and what He had called them to (27:2–4). In fact, in the book of Deuteronomy, Moses told the people twenty-two times to "remember" and to "not forget" what the Lord had done for them. You see, God honors the small steps; He sees them all and reminds us to recall them as we move forward. It is important to celebrate the small wins just as much as the large ones. As I think back, all my cupcake moments are meter stones. Franje's diagnosis that eventually led me to my husband is a meter stone. Being picked up by *that girl* is a meter stone. Each of these moments is an opportunity to reflect on the work God has done in my life that fuels me to keep going!

The author of Psalm 77:11–12 wrote, "I will remember the deeds of the LORD; yes, I will remember your miracles of long ago. I will consider all your works and meditate on all your mighty deeds." That's the posture of an eternal perspective. Not forgetting the past, but letting the "deeds of the LORD" serve as an encouragement of the One running with you! There are obstacles that we will all have to overcome, but you did not come this far to only come this far. As the Israelites experienced, we can do nothing for God. But we can do all things *through* Him who strengthens us! Christ gives us new life. He makes a way when things seem impossible. He helps us overcome when we fall short. I believe every step and every small win is a victory and an opportunity to *remember the meter stones.* So keep taking those baby steps and celebrate every small win. They add up to being the big wins in life.

3. An Eternal Perspective Pursues the Person, Not the Treasure

In 2010, an eighty-year-old art collector named Forrest Fenn announced he'd hidden a treasure worth two million dollars in the Rocky Mountains. It was said that the treasure contained rare nineteenth-century coins, gold nuggets, elaborate jewels, pre-Colombian artifacts, and more inside a small bronze chest. The only hints he provided about the treasure's location were contained in his self-published memoir, *The Thrill of the Chase*. In it he included a twenty-four-line poem full of clues.

Pretty crazy, right?! My detective instincts are kickin' in! It's as if we stepped right into a Nicolas Cage movie! Now, I'm not sure how much I would've gathered from that poem, but over the next decade, more than 350,000 people went searching for that treasure. Some quit their jobs. Some went bankrupt. And five people even died in the pursuit of it.[11] Fast-forward to June 6, 2020, and thirty-two-year-old medical student Jack Stuef cracked the code and found Fenn's treasure!

Stuef himself spent over two years looking for it. He hunted solo, never discussed his search with others, and stayed away from blogs that could lead him astray. When asked how he found it, Stuef said the key to his success was simple: *understand the person of Forrest Fenn.*

"I understood him by reading his words and listening to him talk over and over and over again. And seeking out anything I could get my hands on that told me who he was."[12] To paraphrase Stuef: the treasure was tied to the person.

There's something so simply profound here.

Life is a treasure hunt. There's adventure and there's tragedy. There's thrill and there's disappointment. We tend to chase after things to fill a void inside of us that we can't quite explain. The chasing, and sometimes even the obtaining, is an exercise in futility because if we truly understood the eternal perspective, we'd understand that the treasure is tied to Jesus.

We've all been there. We've all chased after something we thought we wanted or even thought we needed, only to catch it and realize it wasn't all we imagined. Friend, at this point I trust that you know how badly I wanted that Miss Universe crown. Truthfully, there's a giant part of me that believed I needed it to be valuable and worthy and to have a successful future. Of course, having the title opened many once-in-a-lifetime opportunities, yet neither that beautiful crown nor my crowning moment were lasting—just like a bundle of celery leaves that the special drawer in my refrigerator can't keep fresh forever. What we, as believers, have to realize is that the only real treasure that will fill the void in our souls is Jesus. If we want to understand how to find that eternal treasure, we have to get to know Him. We do that through searching Scripture for His words.

True treasure is not in the perishable crowns made of celery, or even those made of pearls and gold, but in the eternal crown of God's love, purpose, and significance.

In the quiet echoes of a church's stage, I had once grappled with my own sense of worthiness as I struggled to answer not only the interviewer's questions regarding identity, value, and confidence, but my own questions too. I had squeezed Tim's hand hoping he could answer the question for me. He couldn't. That was my battle to fight. On that stage, in God's house, I found a truth that glimmered brighter than the Miss Universe stage or crown ever had. It was a moment of divine clarity:

My crown was never taken away from me. I let the loss of my Miss Universe crown replace the value of my eternal crown. The crown I sought wasn't lost; it was simply misplaced.

I misplaced it in the unanswered questions I had around Franje's diagnosis.

I misplaced it in the pressure I put on myself to always continue to reach the same heights of a Miss Universe.

I misplaced it in the misunderstood labels that were given to me by others.

I misplaced it in the guilt that stemmed from confusing my waiting season for a wasted season.

I misplaced it in the fear of feeling like I had no significant impact.

I misplaced it in my rattled faith.

In that moment, I found peace in a profound revelation. The Lord showed up in one of the moments where I felt the least worthy and answered not just the interviewer's questions but my own questions: *What is my value? How much am I worth? Where should my confidence originate from?* In a moment where I had been searching for the treasure, God reminded me that *I am the treasure*. I am His treasure. You are His treasure. He sacrificed everything so that He can spend eternity with you and me. I finally began accepting the truth that as an image-bearer of God, I have been crowned with honor and glory even before I was born (Psalm 8:5).

Just as my mother always helps me find my missing keys, phone, pen, and books, God helped me identify my eternal crown and made sure it was safely placed back on my head. My hope is that this book might have done the same for you. Even if it doesn't magically fill all the holes in your life, I hope rediscovering your eternal crown reminds you of what truly matters: your personal relationship with the King of the universe.

Perhaps my eternal crown was dusty and a little rusty when I found it again, missing pieces here and there. That would change over time. God knew that I wasn't ready to carry the weight of all the crown's jewels just yet. The jewels of understanding the full picture; making sense of the unexplainable; healing from the hurt of loss, of pain from other people, and that my own failures caused; the sadness of losing my sister; the uncertainty of my God-given purpose. As I've grown and deepened my relationship with Him, in God's perfect timing, when I was ready to receive them, one by one God has replenished my crown's jewels.

One by one, I've learned the purpose in the pain, the triumph in the trials, the message in the mess. I know that I won't have a perfectly bejeweled crown where everything is understood, clear, and perfect until the day I get to meet my Maker. And I am okay with that because I have already glimpsed just how glorious, trustworthy, and true all the works of His hands are.

And you, my sweet sister? You are not your flimsy little label that will never stick properly either. You are a daughter of the one true King, royalty waiting to be welcomed home to receive your own eternal crown. A crown made up of a lifetime of your faith being refined "of greater worth than gold, which perishes even though refined by fire—may result in praise, glory and honor when Jesus Christ is revealed" (1 Peter 1:7). Amen.

FLOURISH

IN YOUR OWN LIFE

You made it! Welcome to the last *Your Turn* portion of this book. What do digging, planting, and growing have to do with each other? That's right, flourishing. It's time to bloom, not as a perfect woman, but as someone who is both anchored in the present and shines a spotlight on eternity.

CHECKLIST

My hope for you in Part 4 of the book was to:

- Understand the benefits of being all-in and focused on a task at hand.

- Learn practical ways to stay engaged in the present moment.
- Live by the principle that perfection is overrated, a waste of time, and impossible.
- Reflect on how your current goals, dreams, and priorities align with eternal significance.
- Feel ignited to run hard after what God has called you to.

RECAP

In chapter 9, through my wedding story and the biblical example of the prophet Daniel, you learned about the importance of excellence over perfection. I also shared the power of being present. In the final chapter of this book, I talked about the significance of maintaining an eternal perspective in everything we do.

THE BIG PICTURE

Excellence is not synonymous with perfection. Aiming for excellence means focusing on doing your best every day, all day long. It's a continual pursuit to improve your skills, refine your abilities, and work hard not to repeat mistakes. When you strive for excellence as a parent, as a student, as a business owner, or as an influencer, you set high yet attainable standards by which to measure your work and your progress. You constantly endeavor to be a better you.

Excellence is essential as a Christ follower. Not so you can boast and post about your high-level discipline or hard work or to stay ahead of everyone in this race of life. It's actually not about you at all. Paul wrote in Colossians 3:17, "Whatever you do in word or deed, do all in the name of the Lord Jesus, giving thanks through

Him to God the Father" (NASB1995). When you love, serve, perform, practice, study, or even do seemingly trivial tasks like laundry or making the bed, do it as to the Lord. He is our motivation.

One of the best ways I learned to do this is by staying engaged in the moment. When you're looking ahead at the next thing on your list or are focused on something else you'd rather be doing, you lose the miracle in the moment. You can't do your best or stay present because you're plugged into tomorrow, or next week, or even something that happened weeks ago.

What does it mean to be present? It's simple. Be aware of your surroundings. Look at the person who is talking to you. Listen more than babble. Rein in your thoughts instead of allowing your mind to wander. Notice the colors, smells, and noises around you. Breathe. When you tune into what's happening right now, you become more aware of what you're doing and why. And this type of awareness is what sparks purposeful living.

When Paul wrote his first letter to the church in Corinth, he knew the Christians reading it would understand his athletic references (racing, runners, prize, training, games). Located less than ten miles from Corinth was the city of Isthmia, which was known for hosting the Isthmian Games. Participants who won received a crown of withered pine or celery leaves. Paul described this type of crown as "perishable." And he's right. In 1 Corinthians 9:25, the apostle told the people of Corinth to stop chasing after temporary achievements and instead pursue a crown that lasts. What does that mean? An eternal crown embodies God-confidence, the knowledge of who you are in Him, the use of your skills, abilities, and experiences to reach others with the hope of Christ, surrendering your pain to Him to use for His glory, and being obedient as you follow Him. When you wear a crown that lasts, you live with purpose in a way that expands the kingdom of God. And that's always worth it!

READ, REFLECT, AND ANSWER

One way to honor God is to do our very best in everything we do, from the big things all the way down to the little things.

How do you define excellence?

What are two areas in your life that could use an excellence boost?

What is one thing you can do, starting today, to foster an environment of excellence?

Today's society has created a culture of distraction. It's difficult not to feel the pressure of being constantly connected with the non-stop pinging of modern technologic devices, the influx of pop-up ads, and the human bent to doomscroll away a solid night's sleep. Do you consider yourself easily distracted?

Try asking a roommate, a spouse, or close friend for an unbiased answer. If you admit to being distracted often, what distraction holds the number one spot?

What is one discipline you can incorporate, starting today, to better manage that distraction instead of allowing it to control your time and energy?

We were created for more than what this temporary world offers. Read John 12:25:

> Whoever loves his life loses it, and whoever hates his life in this world will keep it for eternal life. (ESV)

Jesus is not telling us in this scripture to literally hate our lives. That message is antithetical to the hope He came to be and offer. At the same time, Jesus reminds us that clinging to a temporary life on this earth leads to a temporary existence. When we choose to live by the purposes and pressures of our society and culture, we won't leave an eternal legacy for God. When we choose to live with an eternal perspective, however, we position ourselves to do things that matter forever.

Read John 12:25 again. How can you live with an eternal perspective in a temporal world?

ACCEPT THE CHALLENGE

Matthew 6:19–21 tells us, "Do not store up for yourselves treasures on earth, where moths and vermin destroy, and where thieves break in and steal. But store up for yourselves treasures in heaven, where moths and vermin do not destroy, and where thieves do not break in and steal. For where your treasure is, there your heart will be also." You were created for a purpose that is eternal, that lasts beyond this life on earth.

One way to live out purpose and remind yourself of what matters most is to put into words the eternal legacy you want to leave. Spend time thinking about and writing down how you want to be remembered. This challenge can be as short or as long as you want; just be sure to reflect on and use the following prompts to create your response.

- What two things do you want your life to stand for?
- What do you want your closest loved ones to say about you?
- Whose lives will you have impacted?
- How did you handle disappointment?
- How will your family, community, or the world be better because you lived out your purpose on earth?

Writing your legacy is the first step. The next step is to actually live out the legacy on earth. Schedule check-ins with yourself every week. Read back what you wrote above and tweak how you spend your time and where your priorities lie as needed.

PRAYER

(Read this prayer out loud in closing)

> Lord, this world fights for my attention, my time, my resources, and my energy. Remind me that even though I

live here, my eternal home is with You. Open my eyes to what takes me away from making a difference. Show me my blind spots. Help me to honor today and each day forward as an opportunity to leave a legacy. In Jesus' name, amen.

ACKNOWLEDGMENTS

To my husband, Tim: You are one of my greatest cheerleaders and advocates. Thank you for always protecting me and for caring enough to call me out when I'm not giving my best. I'm in constant awe of your wisdom, and your intentionality with the smallest things in life inspires me daily. Thank you for having the patience and giving me the mental, emotional, and physical space to pour my heart out on these two-hundred-plus pages. Thank you for enduring my messy bun, no makeup, mismatched socks, and coffee breath through this writing process. You are my partner, lover, and absolute best friend. I love you so much.

Franje, my little sissy, you might never have known this, and I look forward to telling you one day in heaven, but you are one of my life's greatest inspirations. Thank you for going before me and teaching me to look at life with eternal glasses.

Mamma, Pappa, Elz, and Pappa Johan: I am so blessed to have four parents who love me unconditionally and who would put everything on the line for me in a heartbeat. Thank you for your fierce protection and your constant guidance. I am so lucky to call you all my parents. Elz and Pappa Johan, thank you for selflessly raising and loving me like your own. It's one of the greatest gifts I could have ever wished for.

My pit crew, Allison, Emily Camryn, and Hannah, thank you for sitting with me late at night, keeping me company while writing, bringing meals, and having dance breaks in between. You make life so fun, and I love cry-laughing with you in our most delirious, overtired, and overstimulated states. You have the most uplifting and joyful spirits, and I'm so blessed to have you all as a part of my pit crew.

AJ Gregory, who guided and coached me through writing my first book: your guidance was invaluable. Thank you for your insightful feedback, professionalism, and unwavering support. It truly played such an instrumental role in shaping this manuscript. Thank you for the late-night and early-morning phone calls, navigating time zones, and your patience reading my chapters over and over until they were perfect. What a joy to work with you.

To Wyatt Edwards and Carol Gilham, thank you for your help and hard work as my research consultants and support team. I appreciate the care and diligence you applied to every task. You truly got in the foxhole with me when it mattered most and stayed dedicated to supporting me in reaching every deadline.

My whole W-Group fam: Damon Reiss, vice president and publisher; Stephanie Newton, associate publisher; Lisa-Jo Baker, acquisitions editor; Lauren Bridges, senior editor; Ashley Reed, marketing director; Allison Carter, publicity director. A special shout-out to my fellow South African and absolute boss lady acquisitions editor, who made writing this book one of the most fun, fulfilling, memorable, and rewarding processes ever. I loved working with you, Lisa-Jo. Your kind and gentle honesty made me better. Your sweet and thoughtful comments gave me such clear direction, and your nods of approval inspired me to finish strong.

To my whole WME team and especially Margaret, I want to thank you for sticking by me as I navigated the book-writing process for the first time. It's amazing to think back on some of our first conversations and where we are today. Thank you for your guidance, wisdom, and helping me unlock this next chapter of my life!

Leigh, Dan, and the whole maddjett team—I'm so grateful to have such experienced leaders on Team Demi who help me turn my big ideas into tangible things. I can't wait for what the next season of life has in store for us. And I can promise you it doesn't include a record label! Wink!

The Tebow group, thank you for always striving for excellence, never walking past problems, and always being a breath of fresh air. It's an honor and so fun to do life with you guys!

To my two little hometowns, the people of Sedgefield and Potchefstroom that molded a big part of who I am today. To every schoolteacher, coach, and community member who ever gave me their time, kindness, and taught me so much of what I know today, a thank-you will never be enough.

To the girl who stopped and helped me, thank you for teaching me to be *that girl.*

NOTES

Chapter 1

1. Steve Harvey, "Finalists Speech," Miss Universe Organization, *FOX*, 2017.
2. *Online Etymology Dictionary*, s.v. "confidence," accessed January 28, 2024, https://www.etymonline.com/search?q=confidence.

Chapter 2

1. R. Brian Rickett, "Ruth," ed. John D. Barry et al., *The Lexham Bible Dictionary* (Bellingham, WA: Lexham Press, 2016).
2. Despite the deeply patriarchal culture of Israel and the ancient Near East, individuals who embodied God's values held a more respectful perspective toward women. Boaz, for instance, praised Ruth as "worthy," acknowledging her equal worth to himself. Had Ruth's husband lived, he would have followed the conventional path of inheriting his father's estate and caring for his mother. However, Ruth went above and beyond by leaving her homeland, forsaking her gods, and relocating to a foreign land permanently. The women who compared her to seven sons, symbolizing perfection and blessing, were entirely justified! Ruth serves as a compelling example of a woman navigating a challenging cultural context to fulfill God's plan, even when others may not recognize God's work in their midst.
3. *Cambridge Dictionary*, s.v. "willing," accessed January 28, 2024, https://dictionary.cambridge.org/dictionary/english/willing.

4. Liz Mineo, “Harvard Study, Almost 80 Years Old, Has Proved that Embracing Community Helps us Live Longer, and Be Happier,” *Harvard Gazette*, April 11, 2017, https://news.harvard.edu/gazette/story/2017/04/over-nearly-80-years-harvard-study-has-been-showing-how-to-live-a-healthy-and-happy-life/.
5. Robert Waldinger, “What Makes a Good Life? Lessons from the Longest Study on Happiness,” *TEDxBeaconStreet*, November 2015, video, https://www.ted.com/talks/robert_waldinger_what_makes_a_good_life_lessons_from_the_longest_study_on_happiness.
6. Deborah Byrd, “Use the Southern Cross to Find Due South,” *EarthSky*, April 26, 2017, https://earthsky.org/favorite-star-patterns/how-to-use-southern-cross-to-find-south-celestial-pole/.
7. Bruce McClure, “How to See the Southern Cross from the Northern Hemisphere,” *EarthSky*, April 28, 2023, https://earthsky.org/favorite-star-patterns/the-southern-cross-signpost-of-southern-skies/.

Chapter 3

1. Rarediseases.org, “Cerebellar Agenesis,” National Organization for Rare Disorders (NORD), last updated June 15, 2023, https://rarediseases.org/rare-diseases/cerebellar-agenesis/.
2. Natalia Savenko, “The Emotional Side of Unmet Expectations,” pHClinic, November 2015, https://phclinic.com.au/the-emotional-side-of-unmet-expectations/.
3. Helen Riess, et al., “Empathy Training for Resident Physicians: A Randomized Controlled Trial of a Neuroscience-Informed Curriculum,” *Journal of General Internal Medicine* 27, no. 10 (October 2012): 1280–86, https://www.ncbi.nlm.nih.gov/pmc/articles/PMC3445669/.
4. “Compassionomics,” produced by Rowan-Virtua SOM, February 17, 2021, video, 47:27, featuring Dr. Anthony J. Mazzarelli, https://www.youtube.com/watch?v=zHk9uOCDlDI.
5. Leon Morris, *1 Corinthians: An Introduction and Commentary*, vol. 7, Tyndale New Testament Commentaries (Downers Grove, IL: InterVarsity Press, 1985), 180.

Chapter 4

1. Indiran Govender, “Gender-Based Violence—An Increasing Epidemic in South Africa,” *South African Family Practice* 65, no. 1 (March 31, 2023), doi:10.4102/safp.v65i1.5729.

2. "Gender-Based Violence (Violence Against Women and Girls)," World Bank Brief, September 25, 2019, https://www.worldbank.org/en/topic/socialsustainability/brief/violence-against-women-and-girls.
3. "Violence Against Women," World Health Organization, March 9, 2021, https://www.who.int/en/news-room/fact-sheets/detail/violence-against-women.
4. "Thinking of Changing Your Behavior in 2017? Try Moving First," The Society for Personality and Social Psychology, January 13, 2017, https://spsp.org/news-center/press-release/thinking-changing-your-behavior-2017-try-moving-first.
5. Larry Kokkelenberg, "The Real Reason Construction Companies Fail," Pit & Quarry, November 25, 2019, https://www.pitandquarry.com/the-real-reason-construction-companies-fail/.
6. Margie Warrell, "It's Not Failure That Sets You Back—It's Failing To Risk More Of It," *Forbes*, January 30, 2020, https://www.forbes.com/sites/margiewarrell/2020/01/30/its-not-failure-that-sets-you-back-its-failing-to-risk-more-of-it/?sh=6e6392b82684.
7. Warrell, "It's Not Failure That Sets You Back."
8. This iconic Edison quote is adapted from F. L. Dyer and T. C. Martin *Edison: His Life and Inventions* (1910): "I have gotten a lot of results! I know several thousand things that won't work," from "Thomas Alva Edison," in *Oxford Essential Quotations*, edited by Susan Ratcliffe, *Oxford University Press*, https://www.oxfordreference.com/view/10.1093/acref/9780191826719.001.0001/q-oro-ed4-00003960.
9. Benjamin Mays quote from ReadMikeNow, "Natalie du Toit: First Disabled Athlete to Swim in the Olympics," *How They Play*, updated August 12, 2023, https://howtheyplay.com/individual-sports/Natalie-du-Toit-First-Disabled-Athlete-who-Qualified-To-Compete-Against-Able-bodied-Athletes.
10. "Natalie du Toit," *SwimHistory*, accessed January 28, 2024, https://swimhistory.co.za/index.php/sports/swimming/open-water-swimming/natalie-du-toit.
11. "Natalie du Toit," *Openwaterpedia*, last modified January 14, 2024, https://www.openwaterpedia.com/wiki/Natalie_du_Toit.
12. "'Give up' and 'give in,'" *Britannica*, accessed January 28, 2024, https://www.britannica.com/dictionary/eb/qa/give-up-and-give-in.
13. Mayo Clinic Staff, "Chronic Stress Puts Your Health at Risk," *Mayo*

Clinic, August 1, 2023, https://www.mayoclinic.org/healthy-lifestyle/stress-management/in-depth/stress/art-20046037.

14. The neuroscience behind this has to do with the interplay between our dopamine receptors (i.e., D1, D2, D3, D4, and D5. Each receptor has a different function and is found in different locations of the brain). Simply put, D1 and D5 neurons are often associated with motivation/reward and D2 through D4 neurons may become more active when signaling to the brain to stop certain behavior.
15. "Researchers Discover the Science Behind Giving Up," *UW Medicine Newsroom*, July 24, 2019, https://newsroom.uw.edu/news-releases/researchers-discover-science-behind-giving.
16. Over the years, publications have adapted Ford's quotation from *The Reader's Digest*, Volume 51, The Reader's Digest Association, 1947, 64.
17. Joby Martin with Charles Martin, *Anything is Possible: How Nine Miracles of Jesus Reveal God's Love for You* (New York: FaithWords, March 2023).
18. Johannes P. Louw and Eugene Albert Nida, *Greek-English Lexicon of the New Testament: Based on Semantic Domains* (New York: United Bible Societies, 1996), 352.
19. "About Dr. Leaf," Dr. Leaf, accessed January 28, 2024, https://drleaf.com/pages/about-dr-leaf.
20. Caroline Leaf, "How to Overcome Self-Doubt & Develop a Greatness Mindset," Dr. Leaf, March 8, 2023, https://drleaf.com/blogs/news/how-to-overcome-self-doubt-develop-a-greatness-mindset?_pos=1&_sid=c91d61a8b&_ss=r.

Chapter 5

1. *Cambridge Dictionary*, s.v. "CEO," accessed January, 28 2024, https://dictionary.cambridge.org/us/dictionary/english/ceo.
2. Caroline Leaf, "What Is Meaningful Success?" Dr. Leaf, October 31, 2018, https://drleaf.com/blogs/news/what-is-meaningful-success.
3. Stephen R. Miller, Daniel, vol. 18, *The New American Commentary* (Nashville: Broadman & Holman, 1994), 66–67.
4. "Our Story," Alivia, accessed January 29, 2024, https://www.shopalivia.com/pages/our-story.
5. Quoted in *Many Beautiful Things: The Life and Vision of Lilias Trotter* documentary film, written by Laura Waters Hinson, (Oxvision Films and Image Bearer Pictures, 2015).

6. Quoted in Miriam Rockness, *A Passion for the Impossible: The Life of Lilias Trotter* (Grand Rapids, MI: Discovery House, July 2003), 83.
7. Russ Ramsey, *Rembrandt Is in the Wind* (Grand Rapids, MI: Zondervan, February 2022), 197–98.
8. Quoted in Patricia St. John, *Until the Day Breaks: the Life and Works of Lilias Trotter, Pioneer Missionary to Muslim North Africa* (New York: Authentic Lifestyle, 1990), 17.

Chapter 6

1. "Facts and Figures: Ending Violence Against Women," UNWomen, last modified September 21, 2023, https://www.unwomen.org/en/what-we-do/ending-violence-against-women/facts-and-figures.

Chapter 7

1. B. L. McGinnity, J. Seymour-Ford, and K. J. Andries, "Anne Sullivan," Perkins History Museum, Perkins School for the Blind (Watertown, MA, 2004).
2. Olivia B. Waxman, "Co-Founding the ACLU, Fighting for Labor Rights and Other Helen Keller Accomplishments Students Don't Learn in School," *Time*, December 15, 2020, https://time.com/5918660/helen-keller-disability-history/.
3. "Helen Keller's Books, Essays, and Speeches," American Foundation for the Blind, accessed January 28, 2024, https://afb.org/about-afb/history/helen-keller/books-essays-speeches.
4. Anne Sullivan, "Valedictory address," Perkins School for the Blind, June 1, 1886, https://www.perkins.org/valedictory-address/.
5. Mervin Breneman, *Ezra, Nehemiah, Esther: An Exegetical and Theological Exposition of Holy Scripture* electronic ed., vol. 10, *The New American Commentary* (Nashville: Broadman & Holman, 1993), 336–38.
6. Clyde Haberman, "Remembering Kitty Genovese," *New York Times*, April 10, 2016, https://www.nytimes.com/2016/04/11/us/remembering-kitty-genovese.html.
7. John M. Darley and Bibb Latane, "Bystander Intervention in Emergencies: Diffusion of Responsibility," *Journal of Personality and Social Psychology*, 8, no. 4 part 1 (1968): 377–83, https://doi.org/10.1037/h0025589.
8. "Child Sexual Abuse," CDC, last modified April 6, 2022, https://www.cdc.gov/violenceprevention/childsexualabuse/fastfact.html.
9. Marilyn Van Derbur, *Miss America by Day: Lessons Learned from*

Ultimate Betrayals and Unconditional Love (Mishawaka, IN: Oak Hill Ridge Press, 2003).

10. Marilyn's comments in "Marilyn Van Derbur: A Survivor Story," produced by Marilyn Van Derbur, September 9, 2014, video, https://www.youtube.com/watch?v=YUDNs3cSOXU.
11. H.W.L.F. Mission, HWLF, accessed January 28, 2024, https://hewouldlovefirst.com/pages/mission.

Chapter 8

1. Elzabé Peters, (2011), Wenbrief, Rooi Rose, August 12.
2. Matthew D. Lieberman, *Social: Why Our Brains Are Wired to Connect* (New York: Crown, 2013).
3. Leon Festinger, "A Theory of Social Comparison Processes," *Human Relations* 7, no. 2 (1954): 117–40, https://doi.org/10.1177/001872675400700202.
4. Timothy Keller and Kathy Keller, *The Meaning of Marriage: Facing the Complexities of Commitment with the Wisdom of God* (New York: Penguin Publishing Group, 2013), 101.
5. Teresa Morgan, *Being "in Christ" in the Letters of Paul: Saved Through Christ and in His Hands* (Tübingen, Germany: Mohr Siebeck, 2020).
6. Romans 3:23–24; 6:11, 6:23; 8:1–2, 8:38–39; 12:5; 2 Corinthians 5:17, 19; Galatians 3:28; Ephesians 2:6–7, 2:10, 2:13; Philippians 3:14; 4:6–7, 4:19; 2 Timothy 1:9.

Part 4

1. *Oxford Learner's Dictionary*, s.v. "flourish," Oxford University Press, accessed January 28, 2024, https://www.oxfordlearnersdictionaries.com/us/definition/english/flourish_1.
2. *Online Etymology Dictionary*, s.v. "flourish" (v.)," accessed January 28, 2024, https://www.etymonline.com/word/flourish.

Chapter 9

1. *Online Etymology Dictionary*, s.v. "excellence (n.)," accessed January 28, 2024, https://www.etymonline.com/word/excellence.
2. *Online Etymology Dictionary*, s.v. "procrastination (n.)," accessed January 28, 2024, https://www.etymonline.com/word/procrastination.
3. Fuschia Sirois, "Why We Procrastinate and What to Do About It, with Fuschia Sirois, PhD," *Speaking of Psychology*, podcast, Episode 210,

American Psychological Association, October 2022, https://www.apa.org/news/podcasts/speaking-of-psychology/procrastinate#:~:text=According%20to%20some%20psychologists%2C%20the,can%20help%20us%20overcome%20it.

4. Sirois, "Why We Procrastinate."
5. John Piper, *Don't Waste Your Life* (Wheaton, IL: Crossway Books, 2018), 10–13.
6. "Chara / Joy," *Word Studies*, BibleProject, December 14, 2017, https://bibleproject.com/explore/video/chara-joy/#:~:text=Biblical%20joy%20is%20more%20than,God%20will%20fulfill%20his%20promises.
7. Ecclesiastes 3:12–13, 22; 5:18–20; 8:15; 9:7–10; 11:7–8.
8. "What's So Amazing About Grace? Part 1," *Christianity Today*, October 6, 1997, https://www.christianitytoday.com/ct/1997/october6/7tb52a.html.
9. Brennan Manning, *Ruthless Trust: The Ragamuffin's Path to God* (United States: HarperCollins, 2010), 140.

Chapter 10

1. N. T. Wright and Michael Bird, *The New Testament in Its World: An Introduction to the History, Literature, and Theology of the First Christians* (United Kingdom: Zondervan Academic, 2019), 476–77.
2. Jerry M. Hullinger, "The Historical Background of Paul's Athletic Allusions," *Bibliotheca Sacra* 161, no. 643 (July 2004): 344.
3. Oscar Broneer, "The Apostle Paul and the Isthmian Games," *The Biblical Archaeologist* 25, no. 1 (1962): 14–15.
4. Judith Swaddling, *The Ancient Olympic Games* (Austin, TX: University of Texas Press, 1999), 30.
5. Epictetus, *Discourses* (London: William Heinemann, 1969).
6. A. T. Robertson, *Word Pictures in the New Testament* (Nashville, TN: Broadman Press, 1933).
7. Marvin R. Vincent, *Word Studies in the New Testament*, vol. 1 (New York: Charles Scribner's Sons, 1887).
8. Steven Furtick, "Your perspective will either become your prison or your passport. It will either confine you to the way things are, or launch you into the way things are meant to be," Facebook post, October 27, 2015, https://www.facebook.com/StevenFurtick/posts/your-perspective-will-either-become-your-prison-or-your-passport-it-will-either-/1019263861428362/.

9. *Online Etymology Dictionary*, s.v. "perspective (n.)," accessed January 28, 2024, https://www.etymonline.com/search?q=perspective.
10. "Record-Holding Plants," Encyclopedia.com, accessed January 28, 2024, https://www.encyclopedia.com/science/news-wires-white-papers-and-books/record-holding-plants.
11. Sarah Kuta, "You Can Own a Piece of Forrest Fenn's Treasure," Smithsonian.com, November 28, 2022, https://www.smithsonianmag.com/smart-news/forrest-fenn-treasure-auction-180981183/.
12. Daniel Barbarisi, "The Man Who Found Forrest Fenn's Treasure," *Outside*, December 7, 2020, https://www.outsideonline.com/outdoor-adventure/exploration-survival/forrest-fenn-treasure-jack-stuef/.

ABOUT THE AUTHOR

Demi-Leigh Tebow is a founder of The Tebow Group, entrepreneur, keynote speaker, and influencer who was crowned Miss Universe and Miss South Africa. She resides in the United States with her husband, Tim Tebow, and her three fur babies: Chunk, Paris, and Kobe (aka "The Tebow Pack"). Demi is also the big sister of Franje Peters, who was born with a brain dysgenesis and passed away on May 4, 2019. Through her unique relationship with her sister, Demi has found a strong passion for supporting people with special needs and disabilities alongside the Tim Tebow Foundation. Demi strives to bring compassion to hurting people all over the world and be a voice for the voiceless victims of human trafficking.

She also uses her entrepreneurial gift and social media presence as platforms to spotlight ethical businesses that exist to make a lasting impact in the beauty, lifestyle, and wellness industries.

Demi finds great joy and purpose in sharing her life events to encourage and inspire other women. By sharing her own stories, she has found healing and freedom. Demi hopes to be a light for others, guiding women to find their power and overcome their own obstacles. After surviving a horrific attempted carjacking in South Africa, Demi started the #Unbreakable Campaign, which aims to educate and uplift women, teaching them to find strength within. Visiting more than thirty countries to date, Demi has gained an in-depth perspective on various world cultures, which allows her to identify with many different audiences.